Contents

NavPress ⬤

NavPress is the publishing ministry of The Navigators, an international Christian organization and leader in personal spiritual development. NavPress is committed to helping people grow spiritually and enjoy lives of meaning and hope through personal and group resources that are biblically rooted, culturally relevant, and highly practical.

For a free catalog go to www.NavPress.com
or call 1.800.366.7788 in the United States or 1.800.839.4769 in Canada.

ISBN 978-1-61521-129-6

Printed in the United States of America

1 2 3 4 5 6 7 8 / 12 11 10 09

NAV CLASSIC

The Need of the Hour

DAWSON TROTMAN

NAVPRESS

Editor's Note: *Dawson Trotman delivered the message "The Need of the Hour" shortly before his death in 1956. The message was transcribed and published in 1957.*

In reintroducing this booklet to a new generation, our intent is to preserve the original language of this classic message. Scripture references in the King James Version, the use of male pronouns, and references to communism reflect the original setting in which this booklet was written.

❧❧❧❧

DAWSON TROTMAN, converted at age twenty, gave thirty years to vigorous pursuit of the goal "to know Christ and make Him known." Trotman was a man who believed God, who asked Him for great things and saw God answer. The ministry of The Navigators, which Trotman founded in 1933, is one of those answers. He led the ministry until his death in 1956.

Foreword

When Dawson Trotman, founder and president of The Navigators, died in 1956, he left men and women at work in fourteen countries of the world, helping individuals of varied races and languages come *to know Christ and to make Him known*. That work has continued to grow and is now in 103 countries, with 152 peoples and 150 languages.

Since the day the responsibility for the Navigator ministry was suddenly committed to me, I have been thankful for the principles learned from this man of God.

Dawson lived and moved in terms of the Great

Commission and of men — men God could use to get the job done. Some saw him as a natural leader, some as a Christian disciplinarian, others as a man of dynamic vision or great heart. Working beside him for fifteen years, I knew him primarily as a man who took God at His Word and staked all he had on His promises.

In one of his last messages to staff and trainees at Glen Eyrie, our headquarters and training center in Colorado Springs, Dawson drove home what he saw to be *the need of the hour*. As you read it, expect God to challenge you to a greater faith.

LORNE SANNY
April 1999

I think Dawson Trotman touched more lives than any man I have ever known. Thousands of people of many races and languages and cultures have been influenced by this great man.

Many times we bared our souls to each other as only men do who have the fullest confidence in each other. I sought his counsel often.

Dawson was a man of vision. When our God is small, the world looks big; but when our God is big, the world looks small. And Dawson saw the world as conquerable for Christ. No project was too big and no undertaking too great to tackle if he felt that God was in it; his God was big and the world was little.

He was always dreaming, planning, and working out new methods and means of reaching people for Christ. He seemed to have a sanctified imagination that could look beyond handicaps and circumstances and barriers. He planned big things for Christ.

BILLY GRAHAM

What is the need of the hour? That depends upon the person who is thinking about it. If I'm walking along the street and see a beggar with a tin cup, what's the need of the hour? A dime. If a woman is being taken to the hospital, what's the need of the hour? A doctor.

But in Christian work, what is the need of the hour? I started to list the things that we often feel are *the* need — those things which if supplied would end our troubles.

Some say, "Well, if I just had a larger staff." Would more staff be the answer? Today many a minister would like to have an assistant, and many a mission would like to have more missionaries.

The cry of returned missionaries is always for more men and women to fill up the ranks — to them, the need of the hour.

Others say, "We don't need more workers, but if we had better facilities . . . if we just had more office space and more buildings and bigger grounds and a base of operation. If we had a place like Glen Eyrie, then we could do the job."

In certain areas of the world, they say it's communications we lack or better transportation or better means to take care of health. The need of the hour on many a mission field is merely a radio. But if you get that radio, then there's another need followed by something else and something else. Many feel it is literature. I hear that in my travels all over the world, "We just lack literature."

I know of people today who are saying, "If we could just get into a certain place." For years people have been on the borders of Nepal saying, "If we could just get in." To them the need of the hour is an open door into Nepal. Right now hundreds of people are saying, "If we could just get into China." The Bible says, "My God shall supply all your need" (Philippians 4:19). If the need were an open door into China, why doesn't God open it? "These things saith he that is holy, he that is true, he that hath the key of David, he that openeth, and no man shutteth . . . I have set before thee an open door" (Revelation 3:7-8).

Paul found closed doors, but closed doors to him weren't the problem. I believe those closed doors were used of God to show him the open doors he was to go through next. If God wanted to put His hand over the great country of China tonight, He could open the door in forty-eight hours.

Some say, "We need time. If we just had more time." Others say, "If I just weren't so old, if I were young again." People have said to me, "Daws, if I had known when I was twenty years old what I know now, I could have done a hundred times more for the Lord. Why didn't I?"

Often the biggest need of the hour seems to be money. "If we just had money — that's the answer to a larger staff, more facilities, literature, communications, and transportation. If we just had money."

What is the need of the hour? Frankly, I don't believe it is any of these. I am convinced that the God of the universe is in control, and He will supply all of these needs in His own way and in His own time, all else being right.

Let me tell you what I believe the need of the hour is. Maybe I should call it the *answer* to the need of the hour. I believe it is an army of soldiers, dedicated to Jesus Christ, who believes not only that He is God but that He can fulfill every promise He has ever made and that there isn't anything too hard for Him. It is the only way we can accomplish the thing that is on His heart — getting the gospel to every creature.

In 1948 I was in Germany for six days. I had been put in touch with Colonel Paul Maddox, chief of chaplains for all of Europe, and through his recommendation to the commanding general, I got into Germany. I invited fifty German fellows to meet with me for three days, and twenty-five of them came. I talked to them every evening for three hours, beginning to lay before them the Great Commission and the idea that I felt Germany not only needed to hear the gospel, but that Germans themselves needed to obey the Great Commission by sending missionaries.

I gave them the opportunity to ask questions

during the meetings, and every once in a while a hand would go up. I was trying to lay upon their hearts the very thing the Lord laid on the hearts of the disciples when He told them to go to every creature, make disciples of every nation, start in Jerusalem and go to the ends of the earth. One German spoke up, "But, Mr. Trotman, you don't understand. Here in Germany — some of us right in this room — don't even have an Old Testament; we only have a New Testament." But I pointed out, "When Jesus Christ gave these commandments, they didn't have even a New Testament."

Later one of them said, "But, Mr. Trotman, we have very few good evangelical books in this country. In America you have thus and so." I asked, "How many books did the disciples have?"

A little further on one of them asked, "Is it true that in America you can hear the gospel any day?" I answered, "Yes." He said, "If we had that . . . but we can't get the message out on any radio." I said, "But the disciples had never heard of a radio."

They said, "You have automobiles; we ride bicycles." I reminded them, "The disciples didn't have bicycles. Jesus rode a borrowed burro."

Now these questions didn't come up one right after the other or they would have caught on, but they were brought up during the nine hours together. Finally, one fellow spoke up and said, "In America you have money. I work twelve hours a day for sixty cents. We don't have much money." I replied, "The disciples were sent out without purse and without script."

Every excuse in the books was brought up. "We don't have this, and we don't have that. We don't have buildings; we don't have facilities." Each time I replied, "But the twelve didn't, and He sent them out."

Then finally near the end, one fellow, a little older than the rest and with almost a bitter expression on his face, got up and said, "Mr. Trotman, you in America have never had an occupation force in your land. You don't know what it is to have soldiers of another country roaming your streets. Our souls are not our own." I responded, "The disciples lived at the time Jesus Christ lived, and their souls weren't their own. The Roman soldiers were in charge."

Then it dawned on me in a way I had never

considered before. When Jesus Christ sent the eleven out, He let a situation exist which was so bad that there could never be a worse one. No printing presses, no automobiles, no radios, no television, no telephones, no buildings, not one single church, no uniforms, nothing for the vestry. He didn't even leave them a little emblem.

He left them only a job to do, but with it He said, "All power is given unto me in heaven and in earth. Go ye therefore . . ." (Matthew 28:18-19).

What does the "therefore" mean? It means, "I have the power to give you the order, and I have the power to back you to the hilt." He has *all power in heaven and earth* — not just heaven but in the earth; *all power,* not part of the power, but *all* power, which means power over the Romans and power over the communists.

Earlier Jesus Christ had said to the same little group, "Verily, verily, I say unto you, He that believeth on me . . ." He that what? ". . . *believeth on me,* the works that I do shall he do also; and greater works than these shall he do" (John 14:12).

Do you believe that statement is true? Or must you say that for a moment it makes you stop to wonder? Could it possibly be true that the Son of God would say to a human being, "The things that I do, you shall do, and greater things than these you shall do"?

I believe with all my heart that the reason so many wonderful Christians don't accomplish more in their lives is they don't believe Jesus meant what He said. They have never come to the place where they believe that the all-powerful One who commissioned them could enable them to do these greater works. The last thing He said was, "All power is given unto Me. I'm giving you all your orders now. Go and teach all nations and see that every created being hears the Word."

Now we think it is going to be a tough job even with the printing press, the radio, the airplane, and modern medicine. What do you think the early disciples thought about it? When Paul wrote to the Romans he said, "I thank my God . . . that your faith is spoken of throughout the whole world" (Romans 1:8). When he wrote to the Thessalonian church he said, "For our gospel came not unto you in word only, but also in power, and in the Holy Ghost, and in much assurance" (1 Thessalonians 1:5). And He said to the Thessalonians, who were not even as strong as the Bereans, "For from you sounded out the word of the Lord not only in Macedonia and Achaia, but also in every place your faith to God-ward is spread abroad" (1 Thessalonians 1:8).

How did the message go? Not by telephone, not by television, but by tell-a-person. That's the only method they had. It was as simple as that. Everyone was to tell someone else. "I cannot help but speak the things which I have seen and heard" was the impelling force. That's how it spread, and it did spread. They didn't need the printing press, and they didn't need materials.

Over in England they really went for Bible study and memory materials. It was hard to get them to see their value at first, but when they did, some of them felt they were a necessity. One rainy night during the Billy Graham Crusade at Wembley Stadium, around three thousand came forward at the invitation. Two clergymen came running up to me, "Mr. Trotman, Mr. Trotman, we ran out of materials! What will we do?" I said, "Relax. They probably ran out of them at Pentecost, too!" They looked at me for a minute and, obviously getting the point, said, "That's right!"

The answer is the man, not materials. Maybe the greatest problem today is that we try to put into printed form that which should go from lip to ear and heart to heart. We de-emphasize materials, and people can't understand why.

Materials are the tools. Tools by themselves are useless. If there were a young fellow beginning his study of medicine who had all the necessary instruments for a major operation, and an old doctor who just had a razor blade and a plain, ordinary crooked needle and some store string, I'd put myself into the hands of the old doctor for surgery rather than this boy over here with all his instruments, wouldn't you? It's not only the tools; it's the man who has the tools in his hands.

What is the need of the hour? I'll tell you the need of the hour. It is to believe that our God controls the universe, and when He said, "The earth shall be filled with the knowledge of the glory of the LORD, as the waters cover the sea" (Habakkuk 2:14), He meant it. That is exactly what is going to happen. The earth will be filled with the knowledge of the glory of the Lord!

Today more people than ever in a lot of our civilized countries know about Jesus Christ because of radio, literature, mission societies, Billy Graham, etc. But they only know *about* Him; they don't know Him. The Book says, "The earth shall be filled with the knowledge of the glory of the Lord, as the waters cover the sea." How much does the water cover the sea? Do you think that every square inch of sea has water in it? Yes! You have no illustration more complete than "as the waters cover the sea." That's how every tongue and tribe and nation in every single nook and corner of this earth is going to hear about Jesus Christ and His glory.

What is the need of the hour? It is to believe that "Thy God reigneth" (Isaiah 52:7). The rain isn't coming down like you feel it should in order to have good crops. Can He send it if it's necessary? If He doesn't, can you say, "Thank you, Lord"? That's what He wants. "In every thing give thanks" (1 Thessalonians 5:18).

You don't need anything that He can't supply. Is it knowledge? Is it strength? God can do more through a weakling who is yielded and trusting than He can through a strong man who isn't. "For all the promises of God in him are yea, and in him Amen, unto the glory of God by us" (2 Corinthians 1:20).

I want the fellows and girls who come to Glen Eyrie to go away with this thought securely in their minds: "God, I'll never come to the place where I'm going to let the lack of anything persuade me that You are being hindered." I would rather you would go away with that in your hearts than with methods or materials or ideas that we may have to share with you. Because I know the potential of the man who will come to the place where he can say hour after hour, day after day, week after week, month after month, and year after year, "Lord, I believe my God reigneth."

Listen! You have an excuse if you want one. You have more than an excuse; you have hundreds of them. That isn't what's holding us back. It's that we don't live and preach the fact that He is on the throne. And when He's running the show, He will take care of all the props, even the transportation.

I was in Hong Kong on my way to India in 1948 when a Pan American flight was delayed long enough to make me miss my connection in

Bangkok. I inquired if there were any way for me to get to Calcutta. The crew said, "No, not a chance in the world." Then one said, "We do have orders for this plane to go on to Calcutta, but because of regulations this crew can't take it." So I prayed, "Lord, You know about the meetings in Calcutta, and it's nothing for You to work this out."

We got to Bangkok and a radio message came: "We do not have a crew to bring this ship to Calcutta. Your crew is ordered to bring it." Only four people were on that big DC-6, and the other three didn't have to go to India for three days. I arrived in time for those meetings, and as a result, a man from Nepal came to know the Lord, a man who later became a key for getting the gospel to that closed country way up in the Himalayas.

The need of the hour, as far as I'm concerned, is to believe that God is God and that He is a lot more interested in getting this job done than you and I are. Therefore, if He is more interested in getting the job done, has all power to do it, and has commissioned us to do it, our business is to obey Him — reaching the world for Him and trusting Him to help us do it.

The Lord could easily have said to the disciples, "You fellows are only eleven men, and you lack facilities and transportation, so all I want you to do is start the fire in Jerusalem." But He didn't say that. The believers in South India testify they are glad Thomas believed Jesus Christ that he was to go to the uttermost part of the earth. I understand that the Mar Thoma Church, the largest in southern India, traces its origin back 1,900 years to the work of this disciple. Aren't you glad that Thomas didn't say to Jesus Christ, "I don't have a DC-6 yet"?

"Ye shall be witnesses unto me in . . ." (Acts 1:8) not *either* Jerusalem *or* Samaria *or* Judaea or on the foreign field. You are to be witnesses, when you have the Holy Ghost, "*both* in Jerusalem, *and* in all Judaea, *and* in Samaria, *and* unto the uttermost part of the earth" (emphasis added).

Suppose you are a pastor. You have a responsibility to your people to be a shepherd to the flock. You also have a responsibility for people in other countries. You have to be concerned. The only reason you are not there telling them about Jesus Christ is because you're training the laypeople to love and serve the Lord Jesus Christ in your city, your state, and unto the uttermost part of the earth.

I close up with this, a little of the Nav story. I used to have a map of the world that I kept before me. I'd put my fingers on some of the islands — Australia, New Zealand, Okinawa, Formosa (present-day Taiwan) — and say, "Lord, let me win men for You in these places." I wasn't challenged to do this by hearing a sermon, but by a verse of Scripture, Jeremiah 33:3, "Call unto me, and I will answer thee, and show thee great and mighty things, which thou knowest not."

In the previous chapter Jeremiah had said to the Lord, "Ah Lord GOD! behold, thou hast made the heaven and the earth by thy great power and stretched out arm, and there is nothing too hard for thee" (Jeremiah 32:17). Ten verses later the Lord says to Jeremiah, "I am the LORD, the God of all flesh: is there any thing too hard for me?" Then just a few verses later He says, "All right, if you believe me, call unto me and I will answer."

I asked a buddy, "Do you believe this verse?" He said, "Yes." I said, "I do, too, but I've never seen these great and mighty things, and I'd like to." So we started a prayer meeting every morning. We decided to meet at a certain spot, have a fire built, and be in prayer by five o'clock — not one minute after five. We just made it a date. We prayed two hours on weekdays but met at four on Sundays to pray for our Sunday school boys by name and for the Sunday school. We prayed for Harbor City, Torrance, Long Beach, San Pedro, Los Angeles, Pasadena, and the surrounding cities from which I had received calls from young Christian fellows saying, "Come over here and show us how you're reaching these boys."

The third and fourth weeks we started to include cities up the coast — San Francisco, Oakland, Seattle, and Portland. We said, "Lord, use us in these cities." By the fourth or fifth week we had covered every state in the Union. As we listed them we prayed, "Lord, use us to win young men to You in the state of Oregon. Use us to win young men in Massachusetts." Every morning we prayed for every one of the forty-eight states. Then about the sixth week one of us said to the other something like this: "If we believe God is big enough to let us win men in every one of the forty-eight states, let's go all out!"

We bought a world map and left it up in the Palos Verdes hills. Each morning we'd pull this old map out and pray that the Lord would use us in China and Japan and Korea. At the end of the forty-two days, I felt a burden lift. We stopped asking God to use us and began thanking Him that He was going to do so. "Now faith is the substance of things hoped for" (Hebrews 11:1), and substance is substance. It's reality; it's something you can believe in. Faith comes by hearing, and hearing by the Word of God. We claimed the promises as we prayed. These promises were the brick, and prayer was the mortar that put them together.

After forty-two days, we discontinued our prayer meeting. Forty-eight hours later I was in the hospital, flat on my back for a week, and I had a lot of time to think. The Minute-Men idea came, and from that the Navigator work was born.

Three or four years later I was rummaging around in a drawer of the living-room table when I found a little purple card — "Washington, Oregon." In another drawer was a list of names — Les Spencer from Illinois, John Dedrick of Texas, Gurney

Harris from Arkansas, Ed Goodrick of Wisconsin. I discovered that men from every one of the forty-eight states had come to the Savior during those three or four years. God had answered, and these men were being trained as disciples. Then I thought of the world. "Why, Lord, am I permitted to have a part in this?" For the same reason you are.

"All power in heaven and earth is mine. It's mine for you to appropriate." This is not only a privilege; it's an order. He wants nothing less. God doesn't want you to take an island. He wants you to take the world. For what are you asking God? What do you want? Do you want to win a few? You'll have to start with the few, and you'll have to be successful with the few. You *can* be because Jesus said, "Follow me, and I will make you fishers of men" (Matthew 4:19). No man ever followed Jesus who didn't become a fisher of men. He never fails to do what He promised. If you're not fishing, you're not following. You have to win one before you can win five, and five before you can win five hundred. The world is before you. How big is your faith?

The need of the hour is men who want what Jesus Christ wants and believe He wants to give them the power to do what He has asked. Nothing in the world can stop those men. Do you believe that? Do you want to be one of them? You may, but you will have to ask. "Call unto me, and I will answer thee, and show thee great and mighty things, which thou knowest not." Years ago when I prayed for Formosa, I couldn't have comprehended what I'm seeing now. But that's the way He has promised it will be; so when you call, ask big!

NAVCLASSIC

Born to Reproduce

DAWSON TROTMAN

NAVPRESS

Editor's Note: *"Born to Reproduce" was originally a forty-seven-minute message, given to the staff of Back to the Bible in 1955, that burned deeply in Dawson Trotman's soul. It was later transcribed and published as a booklet that has been read by thousands over the past fifty years.*

In reintroducing this booklet to a new generation, our intent is to preserve the original language of this classic message. Scripture references in the King James Version, the use of male pronouns, and world-population figures reflect the original setting in which this booklet was written.

※※※※

DAWSON TROTMAN, converted at age twenty, gave thirty years to vigorous pursuit of the goal "to know Christ and make Him known." Trotman was a man who believed God, who asked Him for great things and saw God answer. The ministry of The Navigators, which Trotman founded in 1933, is one of those answers. He led the ministry until his death in 1956.

Foreword

In the summer of 1955 it was my privilege to meet Dawson Trotman, director of The Navigators, for the first time. My heart was thrilled not only with his vision of soul-winning but also with the manner in which God had used this man to promote a method of first winning an individual, then teaching him how to win and teach others, multiplying the ministry in this manner, supplementing the mass approach.

Through the years I have met Navigators who were trained by either Dawson Trotman or one of his men, and I have usually found them to be people with a passion for souls, a good knowledge of the Word, and something that made them stand out as individual Christians.

From the day when I met Dawson Trotman, our friendship and fellowship grew by leaps and bounds. We spent many hours together on various occasions, and almost overnight a David-Jonathan love grew.

As I came to know this man better, I soon discovered the secret of his power. Early in his Christian life he and another young man covenanted together to meet for prayer every morning for six weeks in order to find God's will in a certain matter. This spirit and practice of devotion was a rule of his life. He rose early to pray and read God's Word. Without this devotion to God he could not have been so successful in his service.

The unselfishness of Mr. Trotman could be seen on every hand. There was no trying on his part to hoard information or knowledge that he had gained in twenty-two years of experience, but rather there was a willingness to share and to cooperate with us in producing a much more thorough follow-up system for the Back to the Bible broadcast.

The Back to the Bible Broadcast Home Study Course, a follow-up method for young Christians, was the result. Different ones in the organization gave many hours of their time in helping to produce this course, and Mr. Trotman himself supervised every phase of it.

Possibly one of the last major accomplishments of this man was his untiring work in making this Bible course a reality. It was a pooling of both experience and knowledge, which we believe will bear much fruit.

Mr. Trotman went to be with the Lord June 18, 1956. In rescuing another person from drowning in Schroon Lake, New York, he lost his own life. How characteristic this was of his lifelong ministry! One man summed it up in these words: "I think Daws has personally touched more lives than anybody I have ever known."

The work of The Navigators continues under able leadership. It was solidly built on the principle of one person training another instead of one person being the teacher of all.

My own life is dedicated to a greater effort than ever before to persistently follow this great principle of Bible-memory work and person-to-person evangelism.

THEODORE H. EPP
Founding Director, Back to the Bible

A few years ago, while visiting Edinburgh, Scotland, I stood on High Street just down from the castle. As I stood there, I saw a father and a mother coming toward me pushing a baby carriage. They looked very happy, were well dressed and apparently very well-to-do. I tried to catch a glimpse of the baby as they passed and, seeing my interest, they stopped to let me look at the little pink-cheeked member of their family.

I watched them for a little while as they walked on and thought how beautiful it is that God permits a man to choose one woman who seems the most beautiful and lovely to him, and she chooses him out of all the men whom she has ever known. Then they separate themselves to one another, and God in His plan gives them the means of reproduction! It is a wonderful thing that a little child should be born into their family, having some of the father's characteristics and some of the mother's, some of his looks and some of hers. Each sees in that baby a reflection of the one whom he or she loves.

Seeing that little one made me feel homesick for my own children whom I dearly love and whose faces I had not seen for some time. As I continued to stand there I saw another baby carriage, or perambulator as they call it over there, coming in my direction. It was a secondhand affair and very wobbly. Obviously the father and mother were poor. Both were dressed poorly and plainly, but when I indicated my interest in seeing their baby, they stopped and with the same pride as the other parents let me view their little pink-cheeked, beautiful-eyed child.

I thought as these went on their way, "God gave this little baby, whose parents are poor, everything that He gave the other. It has five little fingers on each hand, a little mouth, and two eyes. Properly cared for, those little hands may someday be the hands of an artist or a musician."

Then this other thought came to me. "Isn't it wonderful that God did not select the wealthy and the educated and say, 'You can have children,' and to the poor and the uneducated say, 'You cannot.' Everyone on earth has that privilege."

The first order ever given to man was that he "be fruitful and multiply." In other words, he was to reproduce after his own kind. God did not tell Adam and Eve, our first parents, to be spiritual. They were already in His image. Sin had not yet come in. He just said, "Multiply. I want more just like you, more in My own image."

Of course, the image was marred. But Adam and Eve had children. They began to multiply. There came a time, however, when God had to destroy most of the flesh that had been born. He started over with eight people. The more than two billion people who are on earth today came from the eight who were in the ark because they were fruitful and multiplied.

Hindrances to Multiplying

Only a few things will ever keep human beings from multiplying themselves in the physical realm.

If a couple is not united, they will not reproduce. This is a truth which Christians need to grasp with reference to spiritual reproduction. When a person becomes a child of God, he should realize that he is to live in union with Jesus Christ if he is going to win others to the Savior.

Another factor that can hinder reproduction is disease or impairment to some part of the body that is needed for reproductive purposes. In the spiritual realm sin is the disease that can keep one from winning the lost.

One other thing that can keep people from having children is immaturity. God in His wisdom saw to it that little children cannot have babies. A little boy must first grow to sufficient maturity to be able to earn a living, and a little girl must be old enough to care for a baby.

Everyone should be born again. That is God's desire. God never intended that man should merely live and die — be a walking corpse to be laid in the ground. The vast majority of people know that there is something beyond the grave, and so each one who is born into God's family should seek others to be born again.

A person is born again when he receives Jesus Christ. "But as many as received him, to them gave he power to become the sons of God . . . Which were born, not of blood, nor of the will of the flesh, nor of the will of man, but of God" (John 1:12-13). The new birth. It is God's plan that these new babes in Christ grow. All provision is made for their growth into maturity, and then they are to multiply — not only the rich or the educated, but all alike. Every person who is born into God's family is to multiply.

In the physical realm when your children have children, you become a grandparent. Your parents are then great-grandparents, and theirs are great-great-grandparents. And so it should be in the spiritual.

Spiritual Babes

Wherever you find a Christian who is not leading men and women to Christ, something is wrong. He may still be a babe. I do not mean that he does not know a lot of doctrine and is not well informed through hearing good preaching. I know many people who can argue the pre-, the post-, and the amillennial position and who know much about dispensations but who are still immature. Paul said of some such in Corinth, "And I, brethren, could not speak unto you as unto spiritual [or mature], but as unto carnal, even as unto babes in Christ" (1 Corinthians 3:1).

Because they were babes, they were immature, incapable of spiritual reproduction. In other words, they could not help other people to be born again. Paul continued, "I have fed you with milk, and not with meat: for hitherto ye were not able to bear it . . . ye are yet carnal [or babes]: for . . . there is among you envying, and strife, and divisions" (1 Corinthians 3:2-3). I know a lot of church members, Sunday school teachers, and members of the women's missionary society who will say to each other, "Have you heard about so and so?" and pass along some gossip. Such have done an abominable thing in the sight of God. How horrible it is when a Christian hears something and spreads the story! The Book says, "These six things doth the Lord hate: yea, seven are an abomination unto him . . . a lying tongue . . ." (Proverbs 6:16-17). Oh, the Christians I know, both men and women, who let lying come in!

"He that soweth discord among brethren" (Proverbs 6:19) is another. This is walking as a babe, and I believe that it is one of the basic reasons why some Christians do not have people born again into God's family through them. They are sick spiritually. There is something wrong. There is a spiritual disease in their lives. They are immature. There is not that union with Christ.

[But when all things are right between you and the Lord, regardless of how much or how little you may know intellectually from the standpoint of the world, you can be a spiritual parent. And that, incidentally, may even be when you are very young in the Lord.]

A young lady works at the telephone desk in our office in Colorado Springs. A year and a half ago she was associated with the young communist league in Great Britain. She heard Billy Graham and accepted the Lord Jesus Christ. Soon she and a couple other girls in her art and drama school were used of the Lord to win some girls to Christ. We taught Pat and some of the others, and they in turn taught the girls whom they led to Christ. Some of these have led still other girls to Christ, and they too are training their friends. Patricia is a great-grandmother already, though she is only about a year and four months old in the Lord.

We see this all the time. I know a sailor who, when he was only four months old in the Lord, was a great-grandfather. He had led some sailors to the Lord who in turn led other sailors to the Lord, and these last led still other sailors to the Lord — yet he was only four months old.

How was this done? God used the pure channel of these young Christians' lives in their exuberance and first love for Christ, and out of their hearts the incorruptible seed of the Word of God was sown in the hearts of other people. It took hold. Faith came by the hearing of the Word. They were born again by faith in the Lord Jesus Christ. They observed those Christians who led them to Christ and shared in the joy, the peace, and the thrill of it all. And in their joy, they wanted someone else to know.

In every Christian audience, I am sure there are men and women who have been Christians for five, ten, or twenty years but who do not know of one person who is living for Jesus Christ today because of them. I am not talking now about merely work-ing for Christ, but about producing for Christ. Someone may say, "I gave out a hundred thousand tracts." That is good, but how many sheep did you bring in?

Some time ago I talked to twenty-nine mission-ary candidates. They were graduates of universities or Bible schools or seminaries. As a member of the board I interviewed each one over a period of five days, giving each candidate from half an hour to an hour. Among the questions I asked were two that are very important. The first one had to do with their devotional life. "How is the time you spend with the Lord? Do you feel that your devotional life is what the Lord would have it to be?"

Out of this particular group of twenty-nine only one person said, "I believe my devotional life is what it ought to be." To the others my question then was, "Why is your devotional life not what it should be?"

"Well, you see, I am here at this summer insti-tute," was a common reply. "We have a concentrated course. We do a year's work in only ten weeks. We are so busy."

I said, "All right. Let's back up to when you were in college. Did you have victory in your devotional life then?"

"Well, not exactly."

We traced back and found that never since they came to know the Savior had they had a period of victory in their devotional lives. That was one of the reasons for their sterility — lack of communion with Christ.

The other question I asked them was, "You are going out to the foreign field. You hope to be used by the Lord in winning men and women to Christ. Is that right?"

"Yes."

"You want them to go on and live the victorious life, don't you? You don't want them just to make a decision and then go back into the world, do you?"

"No."

"Then may I ask you something more? How many persons do you know by name today who were won to Christ by you and who are living for Him?"

The majority had to admit that they were ready to cross an ocean and learn a foreign language, but they had not won their first soul who was going on with Jesus Christ. A number of them said that they got many people to go to church; others said they had persuaded some to go forward when the invitation was given.

I asked, "Are they living for Christ now?" Their eyes dropped. I then continued, "How do you expect that by crossing an ocean and speaking in a foreign language with people who are suspicious of you, whose way of life is unfamiliar, you will be able to do there what you have not done here?"

These questions do not apply to missionaries and prospective missionaries only. They apply to all of God's people. Every one of His children ought to be a reproducer.

Are you producing? If not, why not? Is it because of a lack of communion with Christ, your Lord, that closeness of fellowship that is part of the great plan? Or is it some sin in your life, an unconfessed something, that has stopped the flow? Or is it that you are still a babe? "For when for the time ye ought to be teachers, ye have need that one teach you again" (Hebrews 5:12).

How to Produce Reproducers

The reason that we are not getting this gospel to the ends of the earth is not because it is not potent enough.

Twenty-three years ago we took a born-again sailor and spent some time with him, showing him how to reproduce spiritually after his kind. It took time, lots of time. It was not a hurried, thirty-minute challenge in a church service and a hasty good-bye with an invitation to come back next week. We spent time together. We took care of his problems and taught him not only to hear God's Word and to read it, but also how to study it. We taught him how to fill the quiver of his heart with the arrows of God's Word, so that the Spirit of God could lift an arrow from his heart and place it to the bow of his lips and pierce a heart for Christ.

He found a number of boys on his ship, but none of them would go all out for the Lord. They would go to church, but when it came right down to doing something, they were "also-rans." He came to me after a month of this and said, "Dawson, I can't get any of these guys on the ship to get down to business."

I said to him, "Listen, you ask God to give you one. You can't have two until you have one. Ask God to give you a man after your own heart."

He began to pray. One day he came to me and said, "I think I've found him." Later he brought the young fellow over. Three months from the time that I started to work with him, he had found a man of like heart. This first sailor was not the kind of man you had to push and give prizes to before he would do something. He loved the Lord and was willing to pay a price to produce. He worked with this new babe in Christ, and those two fellows began to grow and spiritually reproduce. On that ship 125 men found the Savior before it was sunk at Pearl Harbor. Men off that first battleship are in four continents of the world as missionaries today. It was necessary to make a start, however. The Devil's great trick is to stop anything like this if he can before it gets started. He will stop you, too, if you let him.

There are Christians whose lives run in circles who, nevertheless, have the desire to be spiritual parents. Take a typical example. You meet him in the morning as he goes to work and say to him, "Why are you going to work?"

"Well, I have to earn money."

"What are you earning money for?" you ask.

"Well," he replies, "I have to buy food."

"What do you want food for?"

"I have to eat so as to have strength to go to work and earn some more money."

"What do you want more money for?"

"I have to buy clothes so that I can be dressed to go to work and earn some more money."

"What do you want more money for?"

"I have to buy a house or pay the rent so I will have a place to rest up, so I will be fit to work and earn some more money." And so it goes. There are many Christians like that who are going in big circles. But you continue your questioning and ask, "What else do you do?"

"Oh, I find time to serve the Lord. I am preaching here and there." But down behind all of this he has the one desire to be a spiritual father. He is praying that God will give him a man to teach. It may take six months. It need not take that long, but maybe it takes him six months to get him started taking in the Word and giving it out and getting ready to teach a man himself.

So this first man at the end of six months has another man. Each man starts teaching another in the following six months. At the end of the year, there are just four of them. Perhaps each one teaches a Bible class or helps in a street meeting, but at the same time his main interest is in his man and how he is doing. So at the end of the year the four of them get together and have a prayer meeting and determine, "Now, let's not allow anything to sidetrack us. Let's give the gospel out to a lot of people, but let's check up on at least one man and see him through."

So the four of them in the next six months each get a man. That makes eight at the end of a year and a half. They all go out after another, and at the end of two years there are sixteen men. At the end of three years there are sixty-four; the sixteen have doubled twice. At the end of five years there are 1,024. At the end of fifteen and a half years there are approximately 2,147,500,000. That is the present population of the world of persons over three years of age.

But wait a minute! Suppose that after the first man, A, helps B and B is ready to get his man while

A starts helping another, B is sidetracked, washes out, and does not produce his first man. Fifteen and a half years later you can cut your 2,147,500,000 down to 1,073,750,000 because the Devil caused B to be sterile.

God promised Abraham "in Isaac shall thy seed be called" (Genesis 21:12), so Abraham waited a long, long time for that son. God's promise to make Abraham the father of many nations was all wrapped up in that one son, Isaac. If Hitler had been present and had caused Isaac's death when Abraham had his knife poised over him on Mount Moriah, Hitler could have killed every Jew in that one stroke.

I believe that is why Satan puts all his efforts into getting the Christian busy, busy, busy, but not producing.

Men, where is your man? Women, where is your woman? Where is the one whom you led to Christ and who is now going on with Him?

There is a story in 1 Kings, chapter 20, about a man who gave a prisoner to a servant and instructed the servant to guard the prisoner well. But as the servant was busy here and there, the prisoner made his escape.

The curse of today is that we are too busy. I am not talking about being busy earning money to buy food. I am talking about being busy doing Christian things. We have spiritual activity with little productivity. And productivity comes as a result of what we call "follow-up."

Majoring in Reproducing

Five years ago Billy Graham came to me and said, "Daws, we would like you to help with our follow-up. I've been studying the great evangelists and great revivals, and I fail to see that there was much of a follow-up program. We need it. We are having an average of six thousand people come forward to decide for Christ in a month's campaign. I feel that with the work you have done you could come in and help us."

I said, "Billy, I can't follow up six thousand people. My work is always with individuals and small groups."

"Look, Daws," he answered, "everywhere I go I meet Navigators. I met them in school in Wheaton. They are in my school right now. (He was president of Northwestern Schools at that time.) There must be something to this."

"I just don't have the time," I said.

He tackled me again. The third time he pled with me and said, "Daws, I am not able to sleep nights for thinking of what happens to the converts after a crusade is over."

At that time I was on my way to Formosa (present-day Taiwan) and I said, "While I am there I will pray about it, Billy." On the sands of a Formosan beach I paced up and down two or three hours a day praying, "Lord, how can I do this? I am not even getting the work done You have given me to do. How can I take six months of the year to give to Billy?" But God laid the burden upon my heart.

Why should Billy have asked me to do it? I had said to him that day before I left for Formosa, "Billy, you will have to get somebody else."

He took me by the shoulders and said, "Who else? Who is majoring in this?" I had been majoring in it.

What will it take to jar us out of our complacency and send us home to pray, "God, give me a girl or man whom I can win to Christ, or let me take one who is already won, an infant in Christ, and try to train that one so that he or she will reproduce"?

How thrilled we are to see the masses fill up the seats! But where is your man? I would rather have an "Isaac" alive than a hundred dead, sterile, or immature.

Beginning of Follow-Up

One day years ago, I was driving along in my little Model T Ford and saw a young man walking down the street. I stopped and picked him up. As he got into the car, he swore and said, "It's sure tough to get a ride." I never hear a man take my Savior's name in vain but what my heart aches. I reached into my pocket for a tract and said, "Lad, read this."

He looked up at me and said, "Haven't I seen you somewhere before?"

I looked at him closely. He looked like someone I should know. We figured out that we had met the year before on the same road. He was on his way to a golf course to caddy when I picked him up. He had gotten into my car and had started out the same way with the name "Jesus Christ." I had taken exception to his use of that name and had opened up the New Testament and shown him the way of salvation. He had accepted Jesus Christ as his Savior. In parting I had given him Philippians 1:6, "Being confident of this very thing, that he which hath begun a good work in you will perform it until the day of Jesus Christ."

"God bless you, son. Read this," I said, and sped on my merry way.

A year later there was no more evidence of the new birth and the new creature in this boy than if he had never heard of Jesus Christ.

Winning souls was my great passion. But after I met this boy the second time on the way to the golf course, I began to go back and find some of my "converts." I want to tell you, I was sick at heart. It seemed that Philippians 1:6 was not working.

An Armenian boy came into my office one day and told me about all the souls he had won. He said that they were all Armenians, and he had the list to prove it.

I said, "Well, what is this one doing?"

He said, "That one isn't doing so good. He is backslidden."

"What about this one?" We went all down the list and there was not one living a victorious life.

I said, "Give me your Bible." I turned to Philippians and put a cardboard right under the sixth verse, took a razor blade out of my pocket, and started to come down on the page. He grabbed my hand and asked, "What are you going to do?"

"I'm going to cut this verse out," I said. "It isn't working."

Do you know what was wrong? I had been taking the sixth verse away from its context, verses 3 through 7. Paul was not just saying, "All right, the Lord has started something. He will finish it." But you know, that is what some people tell me when they win a soul. They say, "Well, I just committed him to God."

Suppose I meet someone who has a large family and say to him, "Who is taking care of your children?"

"My family? Oh, I left them with the Lord."

Right away I would say to that one, "I have a verse for you: 'But if any provide not for his own, and specially for those of his own house, he . . . is worse than an infidel'" (1 Timothy 5:8).

Paul said to the elders of the church at Ephesus, "Take heed . . . to all the flock, over the which the

29

Holy Ghost hath made you overseers" (Acts 20:28). You cannot make God the overseer. He makes you the overseer.

We began to work on follow-up. This emphasis on finding and helping some of the converts went on for a couple or three years before the Navigator work started. By that time our work included fewer converts but more time spent with the converts. Soon I could say, as Paul said to the Philippians, "I thank my God upon every remembrance of you, Always in every prayer of mine for you all making request with joy, For your fellowship in the gospel from the first day until now" (Philippians 1:3-5).

He followed up his converts with daily prayer and fellowship. Then he could say, "Being confident of this very thing, that he which hath begun a good work in you will perform it until the day of Jesus Christ" (Philippians 1:6). In keeping with this, the seventh verse reads: "Even as it is meet [or proper] for me to think this of you all, because I have you in my heart."

Before I had forgotten to follow up with the people God had reached through me. But from then on I began to spend the time helping them. That is why sometime later when that first sailor came to me, I saw the value of spending three months with him. I saw an Isaac in him. Isaac had Jacob, and Jacob had the twelve, and all the rest of the nation came through them.

It Takes Time to Do God's Work

You can lead a soul to Christ in twenty minutes to a couple of hours. But it takes from twenty weeks to a couple of years to get him on the road to maturity, victorious over the sins and the recurring problems that come along. He must learn how to make right decisions. He must be warned of the various "isms" that are likely to reach out with their octopus arms and pull him in and sidetrack him.

But when you get yourself a man, you have doubled your ministry—in fact, you have more than doubled your ministry. Do you know why? When you teach your man, he sees how it is done and he imitates you.

If I were the minister of a church and had deacons or elders to pass the plate and choir members to sing, I would say, "Thank God for your help. We need you. Praise the Lord for these extra things that you do," but I would keep pressing home the big job — "Be fruitful and multiply." All these other things are incidental to the supreme task of winning a man or woman to Jesus Christ and then helping him or her to go on.

<u>Where is your man? Where is your woman? Do you have one?</u> You can ask God for one. Search your hearts. Ask the Lord, "Am I spiritually sterile? If I am, why am I?"

Don't let your lack of knowledge stand in the way. It used to be the plan of The Navigators in the early days that whenever the sailors were with us for supper each fellow was asked at the end of the meal to quote a verse.

I would say it this way, "Quote a verse you have learned in the past forty-eight hours if you have one. Otherwise, just give us a verse." One evening as we quoted verses around the table, my little three-year-old daughter's turn came. There was a new sailor next to her who did not think about her quoting Scripture, so without giving her an opportunity, he began. She looked up at him as much as to say, "I am a human being," then she quoted John 3:16 in her own way. "For God so loved the world, dat he gave his only forgotten son, dat *whosoever* believeth in him should not perish, but have everlasting life." She put the emphasis on the "whosoever" because when she was first taught the verse she could not pronounce that word.

Days later that sailor came over and said to me, "You know, I was going to quote that verse of Scripture. It was the only one I knew. But I didn't really know it, not until little Ruthie quoted it. When she said 'whosoever,' I thought, 'that means me.' Back on the ship I accepted the Lord." Today that young man is a missionary in South America.

Until several years after we were married, my wife's father did not know the Lord. Here again God used children to reach a hungry heart. When Ruthie was three and Bruce was five, they went to visit Grandpa and Grandma. Grandpa tried to get them to repeat nursery rhymes. He said "Mary Had a Little Lamb" and "Little Boy Blue," but the children just looked at him and asked, "Who is Little Boy Blue?" He thought they did not know very much.

Their mother said, "They know some things. Quote Romans 3:23, Bruce." Bruce did. Then he asked, "Shall I quote another one, Grandpa?"

"Sure," said Grandpa.

Bruce began to quote verses of Scripture, some fifteen in all, and Ruth quoted some in between. This delighted Grandpa. He took them over to the neighbors and to the aunts and uncles, showing them how well these children knew the Scriptures. In the meantime the Word of God was doing its work. It was not long before the Holy Spirit, through the voices of babes, planted the seed in his heart. "Out of the mouth of babes and sucklings hast thou ordained strength" (Psalm 8:2).

Soul-winners are not soul-winners because of what they know, but because of the Person they know, how well they know Him, and how much they long for others to know Him.

"Oh, but I am afraid," someone says. Remember, "The fear of man bringeth a snare: but whoso putteth his trust in the LORD shall be safe" (Proverbs 29:25). Nothing under heaven except sin, immaturity, and lack of communion will put you in a position in which you cannot reproduce. Furthermore, there is not anything under heaven that can keep a newly born-again one from going on with the Lord if he has a spiritual parent to take care of him and give him the spiritual food God has provided for his normal growth.

Effects obey their causes by irresistible laws. When you sow the seed of God's Word you will get results. Not every heart will receive the Word, but some will and the new birth will take place. When a soul is born, give it the care that Paul gave new believers. Paul believed in follow-up work. He was a busy evangelist, but he took time for follow-up. The New Testament is largely made up of Paul's letters, which were follow-up letters to the converts.

James believed in it. "But be ye doers of the word, and not hearers only," he said in James 1:22. Peter believed in it. "As newborn babes, desire the sincere milk of the word, that ye may grow thereby" (1 Peter 2:2). John believed in it. "I have no greater joy than to hear that my children walk in truth" (3 John 4). All the writings of Peter, Paul, James, and most of John's are food for the new Christian.

The gospel spread to the known world during the first century without radio, television, or the printing press because these produced men who were reproducing. But today we have a lot of "pew-sitters" — people think that if they are faithful in church attendance, put good-sized gifts into the offering plate, and get people to come, they have done their part.

Where is your man? Where is your woman? Where is your boy? Where is your girl? Every one of us, no matter what age we are, should get busy memorizing Scripture. In one Sunday school class a woman seventy-two years of age and another who was seventy-eight finished The Navigators Topical Memory System. They then had something to give.

Load your heart with this precious Seed. You will find that God will direct you to those whom you can lead to Christ. There are many hearts ready for the gospel now.

NAVCLASSIC

Marks of a Disciple

LORNE C. SANNY

NAVPRESS

Editor's Note: Marks of a Disciple *was originally published in 1975. In reintroducing this booklet to a new generation, our intent is to preserve the original language of this classic message. Scripture references in the King James Version, the use of male pronouns, and a few Cold War–era references to communism reflect the original setting in which this booklet was written.*

❦❦❦❦❦

LORNE SANNY became president of The Navigators in 1956 after the death of the ministry's founder, Dawson Trotman. Sanny previously led the Navigator ministry in Seattle and served as vice president of The Navigators under Trotman. He spent many years working closely with Billy Graham, directing counselor training and follow-up for Graham's worldwide crusades. After stepping down from his role as Navigator president in 1986, Sanny went on to launch The Navigators' Business and Professional Ministry and serve as a speaker and mentor to Navigator staff around the world. He died March 28, 2005.

"And Jesus came and spake unto them, saying, All power is given unto me in heaven and in earth. Go ye therefore, and teach all nations, baptizing them in the name of the Father, and of the Son, and of the Holy Ghost: Teaching them to observe all things whatsoever I have commanded you: and lo, I am with you always, even unto the end of the world" (Matthew 28:18-20).

"Go ye therefore, and teach all nations." Another translation (NASB) puts it, "Go therefore and make disciples of all the nations."

Jesus came to this earth to be an example. He came here to show us the Father. He came here to take our sins in His own body on the cross, and He came to destroy the works of the Devil. And while He went about His ministry, along the way He also gathered up people to follow Him. They were called disciples.

Jesus was popular. "And there went great multitudes with him" (Luke 14:25). Yet he told them, "If any man come to me, and hate not his father, and mother, and wife, and children, and brethen, and sisters, yea, and his own life also, he cannot be my disciple. And whosoever doth not bear his cross, and come after me, cannot be my disciple" (Luke 14:26-27). He also said, "So likewise, whosoever he be of you that forsaketh not all that he hath, he cannot be my disciple" (Luke 14:33).

He turned to the crowds that were following Him and three times said to them, ". . . cannot be my disciple . . . cannot be my disciple . . . cannot be my disciple." It's as if He said, "I am not looking for crowds; I'm looking for disciples."

Columnist Walter Lippmann once said, "There are only two kinds of people in the world that really count today, and they are the dedicated Christians and the dedicated communists." And *Time* magazine reported that the French communist Roger Garaudy feels that there are only two major forces in the world today—communism and Christianity.

And I know that among the Christians, the ones who really count are the disciples. As a friend of mine, a Christian leader, said, "Lorne, you don't find many disciples. But when you find one, there's almost no limit to what God can do through him."

How do you recognize a disciple? What does he look like? What are his characteristics? Are you a disciple? Am I a disciple?

I have studied seven or eight passages in the Scriptures having to do with the characteristics of a disciple. They can conveniently be boiled down to three marks of discipleship. When you see these three, you have a disciple.

Identified with Christ

The first mark of a disciple is that he is someone who is identified with the person of Jesus Christ—someone who will openly admit that he belongs to Christ. Now whatever else you may think about baptism, it is a public identification with Jesus Christ. When you are baptized, you are saying, "I take my stand with, I am on the side of, I belong to Jesus Christ."

A friend of mine told me of a Jewish man he led to Christ in Dallas. A few weeks later my friend told another Jewish man, a non-Christian, about the first one. Immediately the second man asked, "Has he been baptized yet?" When my friend said, "No, he hasn't," he replied, "Well, he'll never last." It was later, when the first Jew was baptized, that his family cut him off. He had made open identification with Jesus Christ.

"If thou shalt confess with thy mouth the Lord Jesus, and shalt believe in thine heart that God hath raised him from the dead, thou shalt be saved. For with the heart man believeth unto righteousness; and with the mouth confession is made unto salvation" (Romans 10:9-10). An open identification with Jesus Christ. Jesus promised, "Whosoever therefore shall confess me before men, him will I confess also before my Father which is in heaven" (Matthew 10:32).

A friend told me that when he went with Billy Graham, who was to speak to five hundred men at the Jewish Rotary Club of New York City, he wondered what in the world Mr. Graham would speak on to a Jewish club. When the time came, Billy stood up and spoke on "Christ: The Fulfillment of the Old Testament Prophecies." At the close they gave him a standing ovation. He had identified himself unashamedly with Jesus Christ.

On one occasion Jesus asked the disciples, "Who do you say that I am?" Peter answered, "You are the Christ" (Mark 8:29). It seems everything in His ministry led up to this.

But the thing that strikes me is that *then* "He began to teach them, that the Son of man must suffer many things, and be rejected of the elders, and of the chief priests, and scribes, and be killed, and after three days rise again" (Mark 8:31). A little later He called the multitude and His disciples to Him and said, "Whosoever will come after me, let him deny himself, and take up his cross, and follow me.... Whosoever therefore shall be ashamed of me and of my words in this adulterous and sinful generation; of him also shall the Son of man be ashamed, when he cometh in the glory of his Father with the holy angels" (Mark 8:34,38).

Some years ago when I was with the Billy Graham team in a crusade, a businessman came forward one night and received Christ. The following Sunday night he went to a church that he sometimes attended. After the service he walked up to one of the leading elders in this church and told him, "I was at the Billy Graham meeting last week out at the ballpark. I went forward and received Christ."

"I heard about it, and I am delighted," the elder replied.

Then the businessman asked the elder, "How long have you and I been associated in business?"

"About twenty-three years, I think."

"Have you known Christ as your Savior all those years?" the man asked the elder.

"Yes, I have," he answered.

"Well, I don't remember you ever speaking to me about Christ during those years," the man said. The elder hung his head, and the man continued, "I have thought highly of you. In fact, I thought so highly of you that I felt if anyone could be as fine a man as you and not be a Christian, then I didn't have to be a Christian either."

This elder had lived a good life before his friend, but he had not taken the added step of openly identifying with the One who enabled him to live that kind of life. Here was a fine man, but he did not have this first mark of a disciple of Jesus Christ.

When Jesus asks you to deny yourself, take up your cross daily, and follow Him, what do you think it means? Whatever else it means, I think it means to be identified with Christ, not only when it's popular but when it's unpopular. Not only when it's the thing to do but when it seems as if it's not the thing to do. I like the way the *New English Bible* puts Revelation 1:9. John writes, "I was on the island called Patmos because I had preached God's Word and borne my testimony to Jesus."

I once talked to the chief of police of Stockholm, who was a Christian, and discovered he had been a delegate to Panmunjom back when the Korean truce was first signed. He had interviewed some of the Chinese soldiers as to whether or not they wanted to be repatriated. He told me about a soldier who came through one day and gave his testimony to the interrogators concerning his faith in Jesus Christ. There in the Red Chinese army was a disciple.

A friend of mine traveling by train from Finland to Moscow tried to smuggle in three suitcases full of Bibles. But the Russian colonel at the border took rather unkindly to this idea. In fact, he was a little upset. My friend Jack asked him, "Well, what are you so worried about? Why do you get so upset about someone bringing a Bible into your country?"

"It's a fairy story, nothing but fairy tales," the colonel replied.

"Don't you have fairy-story books in Russia?" Jack asked.

"Oh, yes."

"Well, what's the matter with another one?"

"Ay," said the colonel, "if they believe that Bible, then they won't believe in communism."

So after warning him not to preach and scaring him a little bit, Jack says they let him go on his way.

A few hours later a couple of conductors came by and began to engage Jack and his friends in conversation and to sell them on the merits of communism. It wasn't long before Jack couldn't stand it any longer. He began to preach back to them. After he'd preached to them for a little while, one of the conductors pointed to another conductor at the other end of the car and said, "Now, he's one of yours. That conductor, he's one of your kind."

Later Jack talked to this conductor. Sure enough, he was a born-again Christian. They asked him if he had a Bible. He replied, "No, the last Bible in our town was owned by my grandmother. She tore it up into segments and distributed it to Christians around the town so it couldn't be confiscated all at once."

They asked if he'd like a Bible. (The colonel had confiscated only two of the suitcases of Bibles they had with them.) When they handed him a Bible, he wept and kissed it. Then he wrapped it in newspaper to take it off the train so it wouldn't be taken away from him.

I believe the striking thing about this story is that not only was there a Christian conductor on that train, but the other conductors knew he was a Christian. There was a disciple, identifying himself with the person of Jesus Christ.

Do you take an opportunity to admit that you are a follower of Jesus Christ? Why not determine that at the first opportunity this week you will quietly, graciously, but openly identify yourself with Jesus Christ? This is a mark of a disciple.

One morning I spoke to the SWAP (Salesmen With a Purpose) Club in Colorado Springs. They call in various speakers to tell how selling applies to their business. I spoke on how it applies to the gospel. In the process I explained the gospel. After I had spoken, they introduced the guests. One of them was a friend of mine, Will Perkins, a Plymouth dealer. It was his first time there. When he was introduced, he stood and said, "Gentlemen, two years ago I heard a presentation similar to the one you heard this noon. I bought it, and it has changed my life." Then he sat down. I wondered how many Christians would have taken that little opportunity to identify themselves with the person of Jesus Christ?

Obedient to the Word

A disciple is not only a believer who is visibly identified with the person of Christ, he is also obedient to the Word of Christ—to the Scriptures. *"Go therefore and make disciples of all nations . . . teaching them to observe all that I have commanded you."*

"Teaching them to observe all that I have commanded you." Jesus said, "If ye continue in my word, then are ye my disciples indeed" (John 8:31). If you observe it and apply it to your life, then you are His disciple.

Luke records what happened one day when a crowd of people listened to the Lord Jesus preach. One woman in the crowd was probably middle-aged or a little beyond (I'm interpreting a little bit here). As she listened to Jesus, something welled up within her. Perhaps she had a son who was wayward, and as she looked at the Lord Jesus, she wished her son were like Him. Or maybe she had never had a son and had always wanted to have one. Anyway, she spoke up—she sort of burst out—and said, "Blessed is the womb that bare thee" (Luke 11:27).

Jesus' answer to her was significant. He said, "Yea rather, blessed are they [or happy are they] that hear the word of God, and keep it" (Luke 11:28). That's real blessedness, real happiness—to hear what God has to say and to do it.

I enjoyed reading a book by the late Sam Shoemaker, *Extraordinary Living for Ordinary Men*. In it he says that Christians who are half-committed are half-happy. But to be really happy you need to go all the way in commitment. And this means to be obedient to the Word of Christ.

Obedience is necessary also for stability. The greatest sermon ever preached was the Sermon on the Mount. Notice how Jesus concluded it. He said, "Therefore whosoever heareth these sayings of mine, and doeth them, I will liken him unto a wise man, which built his house upon a rock: And the rain descended, and the floods came, and winds blew, and beat upon that house; and it fell not: for it was founded upon a rock. And every one that heareth these sayings of mine, and doeth them not, shall be likened unto a foolish man, which built his house upon the sand: And the rain descended, and the floods came, and the winds blew, and beat upon that house; and it fell: and great was the fall of it" (Matthew 7:24-27).

What made the difference between the wise man and the foolish man? It wasn't knowledge, because they both heard the same sermon. They went to the same conference; they had the same knowledge. They both heard the Word. Not only that, they had the same circumstances. It says that the rain descended, the floods came, the winds blew and beat upon the house of the wise man. The rain descended, the floods came, the winds blew and beat upon the house of the foolish man. The circumstances were the same. One couldn't say, "Well, you don't know how tough it is where I come from." "Well, you don't know what kind of family life I've got." "You don't know how I suffer down at work." It wasn't their circumstances that made the difference. One thing made the difference between wisdom and foolishness. One obeyed the Word; the other one did not.

Jesus said, "He that hath my commandments, and keepeth them, he it is that loveth me: and he that loveth me shall be loved of my Father, and I will love him, and will manifest myself to him" (John 14:21). What does that mean? It means Jesus will make Himself real to him. To whom? To the one who has His Word and keeps it.

So a disciple does more than attend meetings. He does more than take notes. (He does that, incidentally, in my opinion, though I don't have any Scripture to prove it.) But he finds out what the Bible says and does it. Suppose he's going through

Proverbs in his morning quiet time, and he comes to Proverbs 3:9-10, "Honour the LORD with thy substance, and with the firstfruits of all thine increase: So shall thy barns be filled with plenty, and thy presses shall burst out with new wine."

Early in my marriage, a Christian doctor in Seattle said, "Now let me make a suggestion about handling your family finances. Honor the Lord with your substance, and with the firstfruits of all your increase. Set aside money for the Lord before you pay the rent. Before you buy the food. Even when you think you don't have enough money left to pay the rent and to buy the food. You watch. God will see to it that you have money for the rent and for the food."

Now will He or won't He? Well, the Word promised that He would, and He did.

A friend of mine was looking over the family bills, and they looked pretty big. He and his wife prayed and decided that the first thing they ought to do to get out of debt was to increase their giving. And they are out of debt. They proved that God can fulfill His Word.

Another illustration of obedience to the Word

of Christ is in these words of Jesus: "Therefore if thou bring thy gift to the altar, and there rememberest that thy brother hath ought against thee; leave there thy gift before the altar, and go thy way; first be reconciled to thy brother, and then come and offer thy gift" (Matthew 5:23-24).

When was the last time you went and made something right with someone else? When did you admit to your wife or your children that that fit of temper was sin? It's amazing to me when couples say that neither one has ever asked forgiveness of the other. If you don't find some times when you've got to make some things right, you're about ready for heaven right now. A disciple has a conscience void of offense toward God and man.

Let's go back to "Go therefore and make disciples of all nations." I don't know why it is that some people think the day of missions is over. In one recent year, independent missions in America — not the denominational, just independent missions — needed four thousand missionary candidates that they didn't get. Have you ever considered the possibility that obedience to the Word of Christ might mean leaving your business?

Bob Potter owned a supermarket in Oklahoma City. If he and his wife hadn't sold it and gone into the Lord's work, maybe God would have used someone else. But many people have been blessed by the ministry of Bob Potter through The Navigators.

Many times as I've gone around with the Billy Graham Crusades, young fellows have come up and said, "Mr. Sanny, do you know of any openings in Christian work?"

"Yep, I do."

They'd ask, "Where?"

And I'd say, "Right where you live. Your neighborhood. Where you go to school." I find that God usually leads you to the next step after you take this one. That's where you start.

I'm not speaking of going to the mission field because you're so sick and tired of the office you can't stand it, or because the boss has bugged you for two years and any change would be an improvement. I'm speaking of obedience to the Word of Christ, wherever it may lead and when the going is tough. That's a mark of a disciple.

After Moses died, Joshua had the job of taking three million people into the Promised Land. That included women, children, and livestock. God gave him some instructions. You'd think the Lord would say, "Now look, here's how you handle this problem, here's how you do this, here's how you do that." But, no. He said, "Joshua, one thing above all else is going to take a lot of courage — and it's not leading all these people and facing all the enemies that are in the land. That isn't what's going to take courage." Instead he said, "Only be thou strong and very courageous, that thou mayest observe to do according to all the law" (Joshua 1:7).

You may think it doesn't take courage to be obedient to the Word of God. But I wonder how obedient we really are to the Word. We live in a Christ-rejecting world, and anyone who is going to live in obedience to this Book is going to come into conflict with it. That's how you recognize a disciple. He does more than hear the Word. He puts into practice what he's heard.

The Navigators are kind of rabid on this subject. Year after year you'll hear us beat certain drums all the time. One is that we need to come to know the Bible and apply it. That's why we publish Bible-study courses and Scripture-memory programs.

We need to make up our minds that with God helping us and by the power of the Holy Spirit, we *are* going to be obedient to the Word of Christ. That's a mark of a disciple. He seeks to follow the Bible and do what it says.

Fruitful for Christ

So a disciple is one who is openly identified with the person of Christ. Second, he is obedient to the Word of Christ. And third, he is bearing fruit in the work of Christ. "My Father is glorified by this, that you bear much fruit, and so prove to be My disciples" (John 15:8, NASB).

Now it seems to me that there are two kinds of fruit here. First, the fruit of character, the fruit of the Spirit — love, joy, peace, longsuffering, gentleness, goodness, faith, meekness, temperance (Galatians 5:22-23). And second, there's fruit by way of influencing the lives of others for Christ. "Ye have not chosen me, but I have chosen you, and ordained you, that ye should go and bring forth fruit, and that your fruit should remain" (John 15:16).

I really threw a curve ball to my Sunday school class one Sunday morning. I intended to. We were talking about Jesus sending out the twelve two by two. He gave them authority over unclean spirits. They went out and preached that men should repent. They cast out demons and anointed with oil many who were sick and healed them. Then I asked, "Do you think Judas went out and preached to people to repent? Do you think Judas cast out demons and healed the sick?"

Some feel they can prove that Judas was never saved. Let's assume they're right. Did Judas then preach that people should repent? Did he cast out demons? Did he heal the sick? Could he have?

Look at Jesus' words: "Many will say to me in that day, Lord, Lord, have we not prophesied in thy name? and in thy name have cast out devils? and in thy name done many wonderful works? And then will I profess unto them, I never knew you: depart from me, ye that work iniquity" (Matthew 7:22-23).

My point was that we get so carried away with the spectacular that we think that is the supreme evidence that we are real disciples or Spirit-filled. But the real evidence is shown in our character —love, joy, peace, longsuffering, gentleness, goodness, faith, meekness, temperance. We're considering here the character of a disciple.]

I've heard it said that the apostle Paul, before he was converted, would pray something like this every day, "God, I thank You that I am not a Gentile, that I am not a slave, and that I am not a woman." But look at how God changed his attitude. In his first letter he wrote, "There is neither Jew nor Greek, there is neither bond nor free, there is neither male nor female: for ye are all one in Christ Jesus" (Galatians 3:28). Here is evidence of the fruit of the Spirit in the way of character.

This is what it means to be a disciple of Jesus Christ. It includes one's whole attitude, outlook, character, and relationship to others. By this shall all men know that you are my disciples — if you can work great miracles? No. "By this shall all men know that ye are my disciples, if ye have love one to another" (John 13:35).

When Jesus talked about His ministry and what He came to do, He quoted from Isaiah 61:1,3: "The Spirit of the Lord GOD is upon me; because the LORD hath anointed me to preach good tidings unto the meek; he hath sent me to bind up the brokenhearted, to proclaim liberty to the captives, and the opening of the prison to them that are bound . . . to give unto them beauty for ashes, the oil of joy for mourning, the garment of praise for the spirit of heaviness."

Take this world in which we live with all of its glitter, its tinsel, and its veneer. Strip all of this away, and how would you characterize the real world underneath? Brokenhearted, captive, bound, anxious, sad, depressed.

A disciple is one who gets involved in that kind of world, who is bearing fruit in the work of Christ. He shows the fruit of the Spirit in a Christlike character — love, joy, peace, longsuffering, gentleness, goodness, faith, meekness, temperance. How we need that in the world in which we live!

The Greatest Is Love

What did Jesus say was the greatest identifying mark of all in a disciple? Love. "By this shall all men know that ye are my disciples" — if you do what? "If ye have love one to another."

One of the greatest illustrations of this that I have seen was on the television special *James*

Emory Bond. It was an entire one-hour interview with a black man who was an ex-truck driver. He was in his seventies at the time of the interview. Apparently he lived in Baltimore. One night he watched a panel discussion with some of the city leaders, mayor, chief of police, and others on television. They discussed the race and juvenile-delinquency problems in Baltimore. As he watched, his heart was really moved.

The next day he went down to the television station. He wanted to talk to somebody because he had been so moved by their discussion. He said he knew the answer, but he didn't know whom to tell. At the station they had the good sense not only to interview him, but also to videotape it. All you saw was this gray-haired gentleman as he answered questions coming from off camera.

He said, among other things, that when he was a young fellow growing up on the edge of Baltimore, the white boys would throw rocks at him as he was on his way to school. He began to hate white people. As a young man he started working as a truck driver. One morning when he saw the milk truck go by, he thought how nice it would be if he could just have a little milk before he went to work in the morning.

He stopped the milkman, who was a white man, one day and asked him if he would leave him a quart of milk. He said, "No, I don't deliver milk to niggers."

"So," he said, "the milk came, a quart each morning. Several weeks went by and I realized that he wasn't leaving me a bill, and I wanted to pay for it. So I stopped him one morning and said, 'I want you to give me a bill so I can pay for this.' And the milkman said, 'I don't take money from niggers.' So I said, 'Well, I've got to pay you, you've just got to let me pay you.'

"'Well,' the milkman said, 'tell you what you do. You put the money on the fence post.'"

James Emory Bond said, "I thought I'd have a little fun with him, so I said, 'Now I won't feel like I paid you unless I put it in your hand.' 'No sir,' he said, 'put it on the post.' So I said, 'Okay.' And I put it on the post. When the milkman reached out to take the change, I just laid my hand on top of his. And he jerked it away."

Then he said, "Later on, one of God's servants

by the name of Bill Sunday came to our town, and he told how Jesus Christ died on the cross to take away man's sin and his enmity of heart toward his fellowman. As I heard that, I realized that I needed this, and I walked the sawdust trail. And you know, God took the hate out of my heart for the white man. He put love there."

Apparently a few days later, unknown to him, the milkman also went to hear Billy Sunday. He went forward in the meeting, received Christ, and a couple days later pulled up in front of James Emory Bond's little place. With tears streaming down his face, he apologized for the way he had treated him. And this dear old black man said, "I have loved him, and he has loved me ever since."

Now that's what discipleship means. There is a mark of a disciple. Bearing fruit in the work of Christ. "By this shall all men know that ye are my disciples, if ye have love one to another." When we begin to see more disciples sprinkled around America and around the world, what a difference it will make! Real genuine disciples who will turn the world upside down. There are many already, and we ought to be praying for them.

But not only is there the fruit of Christlike character, but also the fruit of the Spirit in the lives of others. Jesus said, "Ye have not chosen me, but I have chosen you, and ordained you, that ye should go and bring forth fruit, and that your fruit should remain" (John 15:16).

Go and bring forth fruit. Paul wrote to the Romans of his desire: "That I might have some fruit among you also" (Romans 1:13). I think he meant lives influenced for Christ.

Once while I was thinking about this, two events took place that drove the truth home to me. One was something I read about Dr. Charles F. McKoy of Oyster Bay, Long Island. After fifty years of fruitful ministry as a pastor and evangelist, this seventy-one-year-old bachelor began looking around for a retirement home. A bishop from India came to his church to plead for missionary help for India. Dr. McKoy prayed earnestly that God might lay it on the heart of someone in the congregation to respond to this call and go to India. After the third message the bishop turned to Dr. McKoy and said, "I don't think God is looking for someone in the congregation. I think he is looking for the man in the pulpit."

Dr. McKoy could hardly believe his ears. He said, "Bishop, are you losing your mind? I'm seventy-one, I've never been overseas; I've never been on the ocean. The thought of flying terrifies me." But soon a new missionary was on his way to India, green and seasick, but on his way — at age seventy-one. Fifteen years later Dr. McKoy died. Between the ages of seventy-one and eighty-six he had gone around the world nine or ten times winning people to Christ in India and Hong Kong, in the opium dens and in the most difficult places. He was a real disciple in old age also. And I think one reason it struck me was that I was reading in Psalm 92:14, "They shall still bring forth fruit in old age, they shall be fat and flourishing." Your life can be fruitful to the very end.

The same week, we received word from Virginia that a young fellow named Teed Radin, twenty-three years of age and a graduate of Virginia Polytechnic Institute, who would soon be on the Navigator staff, had been in a head-on collision. Teed was killed instantly, and his fiancée died within the hour. One of the fellows wrote that while at V.P.I. Teed had led twenty-five to thirty men to Christ. Among them, five were dedicated, trained, effective men of the cross who, according to this person, would be willing at a moment's notice to die for the cause of Christ.

Dr. McKoy — an old man, a disciple to the end. Teed Radin — a young man, a disciple early in life. In fact, there's no better time to become a disciple than right now. But deep down in our hearts — that's where real business is done with God — we must determine that by God's grace and with the help of the Holy Spirit, we will be true followers of Jesus Christ.

Let's ask ourselves, Am I a true disciple?

Am I willing to be openly identified with the person of Jesus Christ?

Am I seeking to be obedient to the Word of Christ in my everyday life?

Am I bearing fruit in the work of Christ — by way of Christlike character and by influencing the lives of others?

I want to be a disciple. I want to have these marks and characteristics in my life. The only thing I'd like to do beyond that is to help make disciples and to get them to help make others. That's what Jesus wants done. *"Go therefore and make disciples of all nations."*

NAVCLASSIC

How to Spend a Day in Prayer

LORNE C. SANNY

NAVPRESS

Editor's Note: How to Spend a Day in Prayer *was originally published in 1962. In reintroducing this booklet to a new generation, our intent is to preserve the original language of this classic message. The use of male pronouns reflects the original setting in which this booklet was written.*

❧❧❧❧

LORNE SANNY became president of The Navigators in 1956 after the death of the ministry's founder, Dawson Trotman. Sanny previously led the Navigator ministry in Seattle and served as vice president of The Navigators under Trotman. He spent many years working closely with Billy Graham, directing counselor training and follow-up for Graham's worldwide crusades. After stepping down from his role as Navigator president in 1986, Sanny went on to launch The Navigators' Business and Professional Ministry and serve as a speaker and mentor to Navigator staff around the world. He died March 28, 2005.

"Avail yourself of the greatest privilege this side of heaven. Jesus Christ died to make this communion with the Father possible."

— BILLY GRAHAM

"Prayer is a powerful thing, for God has bound and tied Himself thereto."

— MARTIN LUTHER

"God's acquaintance is not made hurriedly. He does not bestow His gifts on the casual or hasty comer and goer. To be much alone with God is the secret of knowing Him and of influence with Him."

— E. M. BOUNDS

"I never thought a day could make such a difference," a friend said to me. "My relationship to everyone seems improved."

"Why don't I do it more often?"

Comments like these come from those who set aside a personal day of prayer.

With so many activities—important ones—clamoring for our time, real prayer is considered more a luxury than a necessity. How much more so spending a *day* in prayer!

The Bible gives us three time-guides for personal prayer. There is the command to "pray without ceasing"—the spirit of prayer—keeping so in tune with God that we can lift our hearts in request or praise anytime through the day.

There is also the practice of a quiet time or morning watch — seen in the life of David (Psalm 5:3), of Daniel (6:10), and of the Lord Jesus (Mark 1:35). This daily time specified for meditation in the Word of God and prayer is indispensable to the growing, healthy Christian.

Then there are examples in the Scripture of extended time given to prayer alone. Jesus spent whole nights praying. Nehemiah prayed "certain days" upon hearing of the plight of Jerusalem. Three times Moses spent forty days and forty nights alone with God.

Learning from God

I believe it was in these special times of prayer that God made known His ways and His plans to Moses (Psalm 103:7). He allowed Moses to look through a chink in the fence and gain special insights, while the rank-and-file Israelites saw only the *acts* of God as they unfolded day by day.

Once I remarked to Dawson Trotman, founder of The Navigators, "You impress me as one who feels he is a man of destiny, one destined to be used of God."

"I don't think that's the case," he replied, "but I know this. God *has* given me some promises that I know He will fulfill." During earlier years Daws spent countless protracted time alone with God, and out of these times the Navigator work grew — not by methods or principles but by promises given to him from the Word.

In my own life one of the most refreshing and stabilizing factors, as well as the means for new direction or confirmation of the will of God, has been those extended times of prayer — in the neighborhood park in Seattle, on a hill behind the Navigator home in Southern California, or out in the Garden of the Gods here in Colorado Springs.

These special prayer times can become anchor points in your life, times when you "drive a stake" as a landmark and go on from there. Your daily quiet time is more effective as you pray into day-by-day reality some of the things the Lord speaks to your heart in protracted times of prayer. The quiet time, in turn, is the foundation for "praying without ceasing," going through the day in communion with God.

Perhaps you haven't spent a protracted time in

prayer because you haven't recognized the need for it. Or maybe you aren't sure what you would do with a whole day on your hands *just to pray*.

Why a Day of Prayer?

Why take this time from a busy life? What is it for?

1. For extended fellowship with God—beyond your morning devotions. It means just plain being with and thinking about God. God has called us into the fellowship of His Son, Jesus Christ (1 Corinthians 1:9). Like many personal relationships, this fellowship is nurtured by spending time together. God takes special note of times when His people reverence Him and *think upon His Name* (Malachi 3:16).

2. For a renewed perspective. Like flying over the battlefield in a reconnaissance plane, a day of prayer gives opportunity to think of the world from God's point of view. Especially when going through some difficulty, we need this perspective to sharpen our vision of the unseen and to let the immediate, tangible things drop into proper place. Our spiritual defenses are strengthened while "we fix our eyes not on what is seen, but on what is unseen. For . . . what is unseen is eternal" (2 Corinthians 4:18).

3. *For catching up on intercession.* There are non-Christian friends and relatives to bring before the Lord, missionaries on various fields, our pastors, neighbors, and Christian associates, our government leaders — to name a few. Influencing people and changing events through prayer is well known among Christians but too little practiced. And as times become more serious around us, we need to reconsider the value of personal prayer, both to accomplish and to deter.

4. *For prayerful consideration of our own lives before the Lord* — personal inventory and evaluation. You will especially want to take a day of prayer when facing important decisions, as well as on a periodic basis. On such a day you can evaluate where you are in relation to your goals and get direction from the Lord through His Word. Promises are there for you and me, just as they have been for Hudson Taylor or George Mueller or Dawson Trotman. And it is in our times alone with God that He gives inner assurance of His promises to us.

5. *For adequate preparation.* Nehemiah, after spending "certain days" seeking the Lord in prayer,

was called in before the king. "Then the king said unto me, For what dost thou make request? So I prayed to the God of heaven. And I said unto the king, If it please the king . . . " — and he outlined his plan (Nehemiah 2:4-5, KJV). Then Nehemiah says, "I arose in the night, I and some few men with me; neither told I any man what my God had put in my heart to do at Jerusalem" (2:12, KJV). When did God put in Nehemiah's heart this plan? I believe it was when he fasted and prayed and waited on God. Then when the day came for action, he was ready.

I heard a boy ask a pilot if it took quick thinking to land his plane when something went wrong. The pilot answered that no, he knew at all times where he would put down *if* something went wrong. He had that thought out ahead of time.

So it should be in our Christian life. If God has given us plans and purposes in those times alone, we will be ready when opportunity comes to move right into it. We won't have to say, "I'm not prepared." The reason many Christians are dead to opportunities is not because they are not mentally alert, but they are simply unprepared in heart. Preparation is made when we get alone with God.

Pray on the Basis of God's Word

Daniel said, "In the first year of [Darius's] reign, I, Daniel, understood from the Scriptures, according to the word of the LORD given to Jeremiah the prophet, that the desolation of Jerusalem would last seventy years. So I turned to the Lord God and pleaded with him in prayer and petition, in fasting, and in sackcloth and ashes. I prayed to the LORD my God and confessed" (Daniel 9:2-4).

He understood by the Scriptures what was to come. And as a result of his exposure to the Word of God, he prayed. It has been said that God purposes, therefore He promises. And we can add, "Therefore I pray the promises, so that God's purposes might come to reality." God purposed to do something, and He promised it; therefore, Daniel prayed. This was Daniel's part in completing the circuit, like an electrical circuit, so that the power could flow through.

Your day alone with the Lord isn't a matter of sitting out on a rock like a statue of *The Thinker* and taking whatever thoughts come to your mind. That's not safe. It should be a day exposed to God's

Word, and then His Word leads you into prayer. You will end the day worse than you started if all you do is engage in introspection, thinking of yourself and your own problems. It isn't your estimate of yourself that counts anyway. It's God's estimate. And He will reveal His estimate to you by the Holy Spirit through His Word, the open Bible. And then the Word leads into prayer.

How to Go About It

How do you go about it? Having set aside a day or portion of a day for prayer, pack a lunch and start out. Find a place where you can be alone, away from distractions. This may be a wooded area near home or your backyard. An outdoor spot is excellent if you can find it, but don't get sidetracked into nature studies and fritter away your time. If you find yourself watching the squirrels or the ants, direct your observation by reading Psalm 104 and meditating on the power of God in creation.

Take along a Bible, a notebook and pencil, a hymnbook, and perhaps a devotional book. I like to have with me the booklet *Power Through Prayer* by E. M. Bounds and read a chapter or two as a challenge to the strategic value of prayer. Or I some-times take Horatius Bonar's *Words to Winners of Souls,* or a missionary biography like *Behind the Ranges,* which records the prayer victories of J. O. Fraser in inland China.

Even if you have all day, you will want to use it profitably. So lose no time in starting, and start purposefully.

Wait on the Lord

Divide the day into three parts: waiting on the Lord, prayer for others, and prayer for yourself.

As you *wait on the Lord,* don't hurry. You will miss the point if you look for some mystical or ecstatic experience. Just seek the Lord, waiting on Him. Isaiah 40:31 promises that those who wait upon the Lord will renew their strength. Psalm 27:14 is one of dozens of verses that mention wait-ing on *Him,* as is Psalm 62:5 — "Find rest, O my soul, in God alone; my hope comes from him."

Wait on Him first *to realize His presence.* Read through a passage like Psalm 139, grasping the truth of His presence with you as you read each verse. Ponder the impossibility of being anywhere

13

in the universe where He is not. Often we are like Jacob when he said, "Surely the LORD is in this place; and I knew it not" (Genesis 28:16, KJV).

Wait on Him also *for cleansing*. The last two verses of Psalm 139 lead you into this. Ask God to search your heart as these verses suggest. When we search our own hearts it can lead to imaginations, morbid introspection, or anything the enemy may want to throw before us. But when the Holy Spirit searches He will bring to your attention that which should be confessed and cleansed. Psalms 51 and 32, David's songs of confession, will help you. Stand upon the firm ground of 1 John 1:9 and claim God's faithfulness to forgive whatever specific thing you confess.

If you realize you've sinned against a brother, make a note of it so you won't forget to set it right. Otherwise, the rest of the day will be hindered. God won't be speaking to you if there is something between you and someone else that you haven't planned to take care of at the earliest possible moment.

As you wait on God, ask for the power of concentration. Bring yourself back from daydreaming.

Next, wait on God *to worship Him*. Psalms 103, 111, and 145 are wonderful portions to follow as you praise the Lord for the greatness of His power. Most of the psalms are prayers. Or turn to Revelation, chapters 4 and 5, and use them in your praise to Him. There is no better way to pray scripturally than to pray Scripture.

If you brought a hymnbook you can sing to the Lord. Some wonderful hymns have been written that put into words what we could scarcely express ourselves. Maybe you don't sing very well—then be sure you're out of earshot of someone else and "make a joyful noise unto the Lord." *He* will appreciate it.

This will lead you naturally into thanksgiving. Reflect upon the wonderful things God has done for you and thank Him for these—for your own salvation and spiritual blessings, for your family, friends, and opportunities. Go beyond that which you thank the Lord for daily, and take time to express appreciation to Him for countless things He's given.

Prayer for Others

Now is the time for the unhurried, more detailed prayer for others whom you don't get to ordinarily. Remember people in addition to those for whom you usually pray. Trace your way around the world, praying for people by countries.

Here are three suggestions for what to pray:

First, ask specific things for them. Perhaps you remember or have jotted down various needs people have mentioned. Use requests from missionary prayer letters. Pray for spiritual strength, courage, physical stamina, mental alertness, and so on. Imagine yourself in the situations where these people are and pray accordingly.

Second, look up some of the prayers in Scripture. Pray what Paul prayed for other people in the first chapter of Philippians and Colossians, and in the first and third chapters of Ephesians. This will help you advance in your prayer from the stage of "Lord, bless so and so and help them to do such and such."

Third, ask for others what you are praying for yourself. Desire for them what the Lord has shown *you*.

If you pray a certain verse or promise of Scripture for a person, you may want to put the reference by his name on your prayer list. Use this verse as you pray for that person the next time. Then use it for thanksgiving as you see the Lord answer.

Prayer for Yourself

The third part of your day will be prayer for yourself. If you are facing an important decision you may want to put this before prayer for others.

Again, let your prayer be ordered by Scripture, and ask the Lord for understanding according to Psalm 119:18. Meditate upon verses of Scripture you have memorized or promises you have previously claimed from the Word. Reading a whole book of the Bible through, perhaps aloud, is a good idea. Consider how it might apply to your life.

In prayer for yourself, 1 Chronicles 4:10 is one good example to follow. Jabez prayed, "Oh, that you would bless me and enlarge my territory! Let your hand be with me, and keep me from harm so that I will be free from pain." That's prayer for your personal life, your growth, God's presence, and

God's protection. Jabez prayed in the will of God, and God granted his request.

"Lord, what do *You* think of my life?" is the attitude of this portion of your day of prayer. Consider your main objectives in the light of what you know to be God's will for you. Jesus said, "My food . . . is to do the will of him who sent me and to finish his work" (John 4:34). Do you want to do God's will more than anything else? Is it really your highest desire?

Then consider your activities — what you *do* — in the context of your objectives. God may speak to you about rearranging your schedule, cutting out certain activities that are good but not best, or some things that are entanglements or impediments to progress. Strip them off. You may be convicted about how you spend your evenings or Saturdays, when you could use the time to advantage and still get the recreation you need.

As you pray, record your thoughts on your activities and use of time, and plan for better scheduling. Perhaps the need for better preparation for your Sunday school class or personal visit with an individual will come to your mind. Or the Lord may impress you to do something special for someone. Make a note of it.

During this part of your day, bring up any problems or decisions you are facing and seek the mind of God on them. It helps to list the factors involved in these decisions or problems. Pray over these factors and look into the Scriptures for guidance. You may be led to a promise or direction from the passages with which you have already filled your mind during the day.

After prayer, you may reach some definite conclusions upon which you can base firm convictions. It should be your aim in a day of prayer to come away with some conclusions and specific direction — some stakes driven. However, do not be discouraged if this is not the case. It may not be God's time for a conclusive answer to your problem. And you may discover that your real need was not to know the next step but to have a new revelation of God Himself.

In looking for promises to claim there's no need to thumb through looking for new or startling ones. Just start with the promises you already know. If you have been through the Topical Memory System, start by meditating on the verses in the "Rely on

God's Resources" section. Chew over some old familiar promises the Lord has given you before, ones you remember as you think back. Pray about applying these verses to your life.

I have found some of the greatest blessings from a new realization of promises I already knew. And the familiar promises may lead you to others. The Bible is full of them.

You may want to mark or underline in your Bible the promises the Lord gives during these protracted times alone. Put the date and a word or two in the margin beside them.

Variety is important during your day of prayer. Read awhile, pray awhile, then walk around. A friend of mine paces the floor of his room for his prayer time. Rather than get cramped in one position, take a walk and stretch; get some variety.

As outside things pop into your mind, simply incorporate those items into prayer. If it's some business item you must not forget, jot it down. Have you noticed how many things come to mind while you are sitting in church? It will be natural for things to occur to you during your prayer day that you should have done, so put them down, pray about them, and plan how you can take care of them and when. Don't just push them aside or they will plague you the rest of the day.

At the end of the day summarize in your notebook some things God has spoken to you about. This will be profitable to refer to later.

Two Questions

The result of your day of prayer should be answers to the two questions Paul asked the Lord on the Damascus road (Acts 22:6-10). Paul's first question was, "Who are you, Lord?" The Lord replied, "I am Jesus." You will be seeking to know Him, to find out who He is. The second question Paul asked was, "What shall I do, Lord?" The Lord answered him specifically. This should be answered or reconfirmed for you in that part of the day when you unhurriedly seek His will for you.

Don't think you must end the day with some new discovery or extraordinary experience. Wait on God and expose yourself to His Word. Looking for a new experience or insight you can share with someone when you get back will get you off track. True, you may gain some new insight, but often this can just take your attention from the real business. The test of such a day is not how exhilarated we are when the day is over but how it works into life tomorrow. If we have really exposed ourselves to the Word and come into contact with God, it will affect our daily life. And that is what we want.

Days of prayer don't just happen. Besides the attempts of our enemy Satan to keep us from praying, the world around us has plenty to offer to fill our time. So we have to *make* time. Plan ahead — the first of every other month, or once a quarter.

God bless you as you do this — and do it soon! You too will probably ask yourself, "Why not more often?"

NAV CLASSIC

Claiming the Promise

DOUG SPARKS

NAVPRESS

Editor's Note: Claiming the Promise *was originally published in 1991. In reintroducing this booklet to a new generation, our intent is to preserve the original language of this classic message. World-population and other statistics reflect the original setting in which this booklet was written.*

༒༒༒༒༒

Doug Sparks's service with The Navigators began in the mid-1950s, when Dawson Trotman sent him to Taiwan. He remained on staff for the next forty-five years, pioneering Navigator ministries throughout Asia, Europe, and the Middle East. He was still actively involved in missions at the time of his death in December 2003.

Here is a truly remarkable little booklet that takes on the toughest, most revolutionary problem in contemporary understanding of the Bible, namely, the profoundly mysterious relationship between the Great Commission of the New Testament and the Abrahamic Covenant of the Old — the very backbone of the Bible.

Furthermore, all of this comes home to the reader in a strikingly personal manner.

DR. RALPH D. WINTER
United States Center for World Mission

M̲y wife, Leila, and I had just returned from five exhausting but fruitful years in Taiwan. We were looking forward to rest — a time alone together away from the rush of ministry, a time of spiritual and marital renewal. Most of all we were looking forward to the birth of our first child, whom we were calling "the tiny world traveler." He was conceived in Taiwan and "traveled" through Southeast Asia, India, the Middle East, Europe, and back to the United States before his birth.

We were finally settled in beautiful Colorado Springs. Each day was marked by the exhilarating anticipation of becoming a family together!

Excitement was also in the air at The Navigators

international headquarters, where a missionary team was being formed to minister among the Mau Mau terrorists in British detention centers. The Mau Mau had terrorized the countryside of Kenya, torturing and murdering fellow Kenyans who would not take the Mau Mau oaths and help them overthrow the British colonials. The rebellion had been broken, and the Mau Mau were rounded up and imprisoned by the tens of thousands. The church council of Kenya had invited The Navigators to preach and start Bible studies in the prison camps.

As I prayed about this I sensed that God was asking me to go with the team. Yet I protested in my heart. Leila was expecting; I wanted and needed to be at her side and share the miracle of birth with her. I wanted to be the first to behold our baby — to hold, to cuddle, to kiss him.

I shared the dilemma with Leila. We prayed; we surrendered. We asked God to let me stay, but we made ourselves available to Him and His perfect will.

We decided not to mention this to anyone but God, asking that, if it was His will, the Navigator leadership would ask me to join the Kenya team, and we could both know His peace in my going. And indeed, a few weeks later I was invited to go to Africa. With His accompanying peace, both Leila and I began making the necessary preparations. It was a tearful departure at the airport. What a surrendered, courageous, loving wife God had given me!

Our missionary team flew to London and the next day to Nairobi, Kenya. The continent of Africa was before us. The Mau Mau terrorists provided our beachhead — a cruel, degenerate, murderous lot whom God loved, whom He wanted to forgive and transform into the beauty of Jesus.

What a response we witnessed to the gospel of Jesus Christ! In the first few weeks, hundreds responded to the Savior, who gave them life and hope where before there was emptiness and despair.

While in Africa, about a week before Leila was due to have our baby, I went out for a long walk and talk with God. I prayed over every detail I could imagine concerning the birth of our child, not knowing that at that very moment our son, Kent, was being born!

The prayer time felt inspired—God speaking things into existence through human lips. From praying for Leila and the baby, God led me to pray for Africa. The sky was filled with sparkling stars, shining brightly in a jet-black sky. They seemed to light up the earth. It was these stars shining in the darkness that reminded me as I prayed of God's promise to Abraham in Genesis 22:17-18:

> Indeed I will greatly bless you, and I will greatly multiply your seed as the stars of the heavens and as the sand which is on the seashore; and your seed shall possess the gate of their enemies. In your seed all the nations of the earth shall be blessed, because you have obeyed My voice. (NASB)

As I was reviewing this promise in my mind, I began claiming it in prayer: "Oh, Lord, give us African disciples of Christ who will shine as lights throughout this dark continent. May they bless every tribe with the knowledge of Christ. May they conquer and possess the strongholds of Satan until the peoples of Africa experience the blessing of God."

God is true to His promise, and He is answering that prayer. Through the ministry of many Navigator missionaries and Africans, God is raising up disciples all over Africa who are blessed and multiplying.

So often we focus our prayers merely on ourselves and our circle of experience. We are like spiritual shut-ins in a world in which God is actually doing great and mighty things to fulfill His promise. We tend to stand on the sidelines, asking God for peanuts when we could be asking for continents.

The purpose of this booklet is to demonstrate how to claim the promise of God in prayer. To effectively claim the promise we should understand the answers to each of the following questions:

1. What is the meaning of the promise?
2. To whom is the promise given?

3. How does the promise work?
4. Who is the God of the promise?
5. How certain is the promise?
6. What is the need for the promise?
7. How do we claim the promise?

What Is the Meaning of the Promise?

In Genesis 12:1-3 we read, "The LORD had said to Abram, 'Leave your country, your people and your father's household and go to the land I will show you. I will make you into a great nation and I will bless you; I will make your name great, and you will be a blessing. I will bless those who bless you, and whoever curses you I will curse; and all peoples on earth will be blessed through you.'"

It is encouraging to our faith to see that God *has* fulfilled a large part of His promise to Abraham. From Abraham *has* come a great nation and a great name—he is the father of all believers (Romans 4:11). The nation of Israel *did* possess the land and under kings David and Solomon became a mighty empire. Today, God is fulfilling the universal promise made to Abraham to bless all the peoples of the world through Christ.

John R. Stott, British theologian, Bible expositor, and author, said, "God made a promise to Abraham. And an understanding of that promise is indispensable to an understanding of the Bible and of the Christian mission. . . . The whole of God's purpose is encapsulated here."[1]

The blessing in this promise is salvation in all of its ramifications for every people on earth. Our common English use for the word *blessing,* "to confer well-being, happiness, or prosperity on," is totally inadequate and degrading if applied to this scripture.

The word *blessing* here means "divine favor" in its ultimate sense. According to Dr. Ralph Winter, founder and director of the U.S. Center for World Mission, it means to "reinherit." To be blessed of God in this passage is to become a child of God with all its privileges and responsibilities. It is reinheriting that lost position of sonship. It is becoming a joint heir with Christ. It is also being involved in and committed to the family business — to bless all peoples of the earth.

The apostle Paul gives us the New Testament

commentary on this promise in Romans 4 and Galatians 3. He expounds on the blessing: It is righteousness by faith, right-standing with a holy God, without works. It is the blessedness of complete forgiveness. It is justification through faith for everyone who believes in Jesus Christ. It is being indwelt by the Holy Spirit and receiving the divine nature. Christ in us becomes our hope of glory. The Spirit recreates us with the nature and presence of Christ in our lives.

To Whom Is the Promise Given?

God wants all of His children involved in His plan for the whole world through the promise to Abraham.

Are we as Christians presumptuous in claiming this promise? No. The promise is for all believers. It is our privilege and right to claim it in prayer for ourselves and for all the peoples on earth.

Notice how the New Testament affirms this: "So those who have faith are blessed along with Abraham, the man of faith" (Galatians 3:9); "If you belong to Christ, then you are Abraham's seed, and heirs according to the promise" (Galatians 3:29);

and "Now you, brothers, like Isaac, are children of promise" (Galatians 4:28).

We are children and heirs who can claim the blessing of Abraham in prayer and by faith.

John Stott said, "Who then are the true descendants of Abraham, the true beneficiaries of God's promise to him? Paul does not leave us in any doubt. They are the believers in Christ of whatever race."[2]

God is no respecter of persons. He loves each one infinitely, tenderly, and compassionately. He delights to bless each people, each believer. It is His nature to do so. He is the Father and originator of loving-kindness, graciousness, mercy, and generosity. He is the very essence of "I will bless you."

The Father's purpose is not just to bless you but to extend the blessing through you to the peoples of the earth. The other side of the coin in blessing is sharing. After the promise "I will bless you" comes the divine imperative "You will be a blessing."

In God's creation, He generates seed-bearing plants, fish, birds, animals, humans — all with their own unique seed to reproduce after their kind. God commands them in Genesis 1 to be fruitful and multiply and fill the earth.

God's plan in re-creation is similar. In Genesis 22:18 God tells Abraham, "In thy seed shall all the nations of the earth be blessed" (KJV). Paul points out that this *seed* is Jesus Christ (Galatians 3:16).

So each believer is carrying about the seed of Jesus Christ to reproduce in another. God promises, "I will greatly bless you. I will greatly multiply you."

After rising from the dead, Jesus gathered His disciples and opened their minds to the Scriptures. They saw how He fulfilled the promises and the prophecies (Luke 24:44-47). Jesus then commanded His disciples to be His witnesses to the uttermost part of the earth (Acts 1:8). In the Great Commission He commands, "Go and make disciples of all nations" (Matthew 28:19). What He commands, He enables us to do. He promised His presence and His power to disciple among all peoples. Having fulfilled the promise Himself, He is able to command us to fulfill it with His power.

Ralph Winter marries the promise of Genesis 12 with the Great Commission: "There is formidable scholarship that understands the mandate of Genesis 12:1-3; 26:4-5; and 28:14-15 as the first appearance of the Great Commission, pointing, as these verses do, to all the nations of the world, to a spiritual 'blessing' involving sonship, and to a mechanism consisting of human intermediaries. Thus, these are the foundation verses linking the whole Bible to the redemptive work of Jesus Christ and His mission to the nations."[3]

How Does the Promise Work?

The promise is claimed by faith. The Great Commission is obeyed by faith. The apostle Paul described the underlying principle: "Therefore, the promise comes by faith, so that it may be by grace and may be guaranteed to all Abraham's offspring" (Romans 4:16). *The operating principle of the promise is faith, that it may be by grace.*

Abraham believed God, and it was credited to him as righteousness. This came *before* circumcision, *before* the Law was given.

But some would say, "Didn't Abraham's obedience prompt God's fullest blessing?"

Yes, Abraham left his country and his household, but he didn't go out "by his own works" but "by faith, responding in obedience," according to Hebrews 11. Later, when God commanded Abraham to offer his son Isaac as a sacrifice, we see that the motivation and power for obedience came from faith. "By faith Abraham, when God tested him, offered Isaac as a sacrifice" (verse 17). Obedience was the result, the demonstration, of Abraham's faith. The condition of the promise is a live faith that *responds* in obedience.

Believing is actually responding to the faith God gives. It accepts righteousness as a gift, and therefore is not consumed with weighing our works to see if we are good enough for God to fulfill His promise to us.

One of the great problems within evangelical Christianity is that we receive the promise of Christ's blessing and salvation by faith, then lapse into trying to propagate this promise by our own works and worthiness. The world task before us requires far more than human effort. It requires a miraculous working of God in fulfillment of His impossible promise!

The key question we have to ask ourselves is, "What principle are we going to operate on in claiming this promise?" The principle of works? In other words, if I will do this, God will do that? The characteristic here is obligation. The result is that I get the credit. I can boast; I can find fulfillment in myself, in what I do. But I can never be sure I have done enough.

Or, are we going to operate on the basis of faith by grace? This focuses on what God says *He* will do, because He is gracious and fully able. I simply act accordingly. I step out in faith believing God will do what He says. The result is that God gets the credit, and I find my fulfillment in God and what He has done according to His promise.

Somewhere along the way, each believer must make a choice. Will it be works or grace through faith? Which principle are you choosing? It is impossible for these contrary principles to co-exist. Paul pointed this out: "And if [it be] by grace, then it is no longer by works; if it were, grace would no longer be grace" (Romans 11:6).

This indelible lesson was brought home to me when I was working in Europe. One day a young, newly married friend came into my office in London. She was in tears. Repeatedly she had gone to the embassy to get a visa so she could join her missionary husband in Africa, but the official was very rude to her and didn't want to be bothered.

We decided to pray together on the basis of Christ's worthiness and just because of His grace. When my friend returned to the embassy that same day, the same official cordially granted her visa. He even offered to call the airport for her!

It is *by His grace* that we have boldness and access to God to receive help for every need. We are confident, free, and motivated, then, to do the work of prayer—both for ourselves and for the unreached peoples of the world.

Never mind that we find our faith small compared to Abraham's. The criterion is not the strength of our faith but the focus of it. For our faith to grow we must grow in the knowledge of the object of our faith—God Himself.

Who Is the God of the Promise?

In the promise of Genesis 12:1-3, either directly expressed or indirectly, God the Father says seven times, "I will." Who is this God who says, "I will"?

To Abram God reveals Himself as El Shaddai, the God "I will" in Genesis 17:1. At this point,

Abram was ninety-nine years old. According to Scripture, Sarai's womb was dead. It was physically impossible for Abram and Sarai to have a son. But it is when we humans are hopeless that we can best see who the God of promise really is and what He can do for us. *El Shaddai* means "the Lord almighty," "the Lord all sufficient," the God of infinite power and supply.

The object of our faith and prayer is God. What we ask for — how we pray — is determined by our concept of who He is. To pray in truth we must know the promise. To pray in power we must know the God of promise.

Paul gives us some rich insights into the implications of El Shaddai in Romans 4:17 — "God, who gives life to the dead and calls into being that which does not exist" (NASB). And in verses 18-21 we see Abraham's response in faith to that revelation of God:

> Against all hope, Abraham
> in hope believed ... just as it
> had been said to him. ... He
> faced the fact that his body

was as good as dead.... He did not waver through unbelief regarding the promise of God, but was strengthened in his faith and gave glory to God, being fully persuaded that God [El Shaddai] had power to do what he had promised.

Imagine an old man of ninety-nine having his name changed from Abram, meaning "Barren Exalted One" (which certainly described him), to Abraham, "the Father of a Multitude" and "the Father of Many Nations"! His friends must have thought he had gone senile! But from Abraham's point of view, God had said it and Abraham was ready to "go public" with it. Abraham believed that God *had* made him a father of many nations. And, because he knew the One who had made the promise, he gave glory to God as though it were already true.

We need to see God as El Shaddai — "the Lord almighty," "the Lord sufficient," the God of infinite power and supply who hears and answers prayer. This is the nature of the Promiser.

How Certain Is the Promise?

In claiming the promise we must be utterly convinced of its certainty. God has said it. Christ has fulfilled it by becoming a man, dying to purchase our salvation, and rising again. Now He sits at the right hand of God to see the promise become a reality among the peoples of the earth. The promise is fulfilled already in the heavens. We need only to pray it down to earth.

The certainty of the promise is based on the integrity and power of the One giving it. God's promise in Genesis 12 was enough, but for our sakes He confirmed it with an oath in Genesis 22:16 to clarify its certainty: "By Myself I have sworn, declares the Lord" (NASB). The promise had already been given. It was true. God didn't have to give it again to make it true. He didn't have to use an oath to bind Himself to it. But the writer of Hebrews told us, "Because God wanted to make the unchanging nature of his purpose very clear to the heirs of what was promised, he confirmed it with an oath" (Hebrews 6:17).

An oath is like a contract. When you sign a contract you are taking an oath that you will do certain things. This is a long-standing, universal practice. God gave this oath (and He could swear by no greater One than Himself) to let *us* know He meant it.

In the book of Revelation we see a multitude that no man can number, from all the tribes and peoples and kindreds and tongues. They are standing before the throne of God, worshipping Him and praising Him. His kingdom *has* come; the promise is sure. In God's sight it is already done.

The key to certainty, then, is to ask God for what He has already said He wants to do! R. A. Torrey, internationally known preacher and author, has written, "Here is one of the greatest secrets of prevailing prayer: to study the Word to find what God's will is as revealed there in the promises, and then simply take these promises and spread them out before God in prayer with the absolutely unwavering expectation that He will do what He has promised in His Word."[4]

Now we know with certainty that it is the Father's will to bless or reinstate us and the peoples of all the earth as His heirs through Christ, so we may ask for it with confidence.

What Is the Need for the Promise?

God's love for those who have never heard is unfailing. He sees and cares about the peoples of the world, their temporal needs, their poverty, hunger, injustice, and suffering. He is deeply compassionate and desires to help them right now, where they are. He also sees beyond the temporal into the eternal. His love is an everlasting love, and He desires that each person on earth be in His family and kingdom now and forever.

God's approach to the peoples of the world is not a Band-Aid approach. It involves all the means of a holy, just, and loving God forgiving and justifying those who have both willfully and blindly gone their own way. He wants to transform them into Christlikeness and to make them all they were created to be. And so God gives a promise for such a blessing and through Christ provides the means to fulfilling the promise. He gives us, in turn, the command to act on it:

- "Go . . . and preach the gospel to every creature" (Mark 16:15, KJV).
- "Go and make disciples of all nations" (Matthew 28:19).

God's promise announces His *purpose* to bless all peoples of the world. Christ's Great Commission announces God's *program* for doing that today.

Over half of the 5.3 billion people who occupy our planet today live in Asia.[5] China is the first country with a population of over a billion people. Some estimate that by the year 2000 India will have a billion people.[6] But more formidable than the numbers are the thousands of ethnic languages and cultures that separate these peoples from each other and from the gospel.

Politically, 85 percent of Asians (2.3 billion) live in nations where missionaries are banned. Christians can enter these nations only as business and professional people, sharing their lives and witnessing for Christ on a personal basis. Christian ministries are suppressed. The vast majority of the peoples of Asia have never clearly heard the gospel of Jesus Christ.

We don't have the ability to reach the masses, to penetrate these cultures, languages, and deeply rooted ideologies. We don't have the army of disciplers to send to them. We don't have the power to overcome Satan's influence over these peoples. The task of evangelizing Asia is simply impossible for men.

Jesus said, "But what is impossible with men is possible with God" (Luke 18:27). The One who made the promise "to bless all the peoples of the earth" is the One who has the power to do it. God's promise and God's power are working today in remarkable ways through God's people to accomplish this task. Today Christianity worldwide is growing at a rate of seventy thousand people daily.[7]

When the communists took over China in 1949, about three million claimed to be Christians. Today, conservative estimates indicate there are forty to fifty million Christians in China![8] Africa, too, has seen a phenomenal turning to Christ. Estimates are that by the year 2000 there will be 350 million African Christians — in only 120 years of missionary effort.[9]

God is on the move. He is implementing His

plan for the earth. We must look to Him and the power of His promise to reach the remaining peoples of every tongue and tribe and nation who have yet to hear of Jesus Christ and the salvation He freely offers.

This missionary task can only be accomplished as we do these things:

- Believe the promise of God.
- Pray over the promise.
- Act on the promise.

How Do We Claim the Promise?

Seeing then that the promise is so certain and so needed, how can we be partakers of it? Our part in the promise to bless the nations is directly proportionate to our *faith* and our *prayers*.

What petitions should we bring to God? How should we pray the promise into being?

In Our Personal Lives

The Lord promises, "I will bless you." We need to pray, "Lord, El Shaddai, You say You will pour forth Your life into me. I want to claim Your love in all my relationships. Pour forth Your love. When I'm tempted, pour forth Your holiness. When I'm anxious, pour forth Your peace. When there is injustice, pour forth Your justice. In my business dealings, pour forth Your integrity. When I'm wrong, pour forth Your mercy. When I'm disappointed and discouraged or depressed, pour forth Your joy."

When we pray and claim "I will bless you," we remember that we inherit this blessing because God is our Father and Christ's nature is alive in us by the power of the Holy Spirit. We believe it, ask it, expect it, act on it. We have the promise. We should pray in the manner of Ephesians 3:20, "Now to Him who is able to do exceedingly abundantly above all that we ask or think, according to the power that works in us" (NKJV).

In Our Direct Personal Relationships

The Lord promises, "You will be a blessing." When Christ becomes a reality in our lives, it will affect our relationships. His life will pour over and bless other people. God calls that multiplying! "I will *greatly* multiply you." "I will *surely* multiply you."

In order to multiply, we have to let people into our lives to see the difference Christ makes—not a pseudodifference, not a way to act, but reality. They need to see Christ incarnated in us. That incarnation presses us into acting on their behalf. As we build bridges of mutual love, respect, and trust, the gospel message we declare will ring true.

I don't believe I would have ever come to Christ through talk, argument, or preaching. Over a period of months I saw the tremendous change and blessing Christ made in an old high-school buddy of mine. His faith was real, his love for me genuine. That is what made me want Christ's blessing, too, and I received Him into my life.

In fulfillment of the promise, the divine life is so poured into our lives by El Shaddai that it overflows and blesses others.

For the World

The Lord promises, "All peoples will be blessed through you." Our praying for the peoples of the world should reflect both the size of the promise and the greatness of the Promiser. The world is small, but God is big. He invites us, "Call to Me, and I will answer you, and show you great and mighty things, which you do not know" (Jeremiah 33:3, NKJV).

In praying for the peoples of the world, we wrestle with the powers of darkness. Satan is called "the ruler of this world," and he has far too long possessed and ruled over these peoples.

The powers of Satan must be defeated in prayer, and laborers with the good news of Jesus Christ must go to these people. This is why Jesus said, "The harvest is plentiful but the workers are few. Ask [beseech] the Lord of the harvest, therefore, to send out workers into his harvest field" (Matthew 9:37-38).

S. D. Gordon, theologian and prolific writer of the early twentieth century, said, "The greatest thing each one of us can do is to pray. If we go personally to some distant land, still we have gone to only one place. Prayer puts us into direct dynamic touch with the world. A man may go aside today and shut the door and as really spend a half hour of his life in India (or Lebanon or China) as though he were there in person. Surely you and I must get more half hours for this secret service."[10]

Many years ago there was a very dedicated young Christian girl in the eastern United States. She was of poor health and could not be very active for the Lord, so she took upon herself a ministry of prayer. She became burdened for a little-known tribe of African pygmies and "adopted" them as her prayer target. She wrote many missionaries in the region to find out more about this tribe. The pygmies were nomads, constantly roaming to new areas. They were very difficult to reach and evangelize, but she claimed them as "her people."

She prayed faithfully day after day, week after week, year after year. Eventually her health worsened and she died.

Twenty years later, Gospel Recordings, a specialized mission agency, rediscovered this tribe. Using interpreters, their missionaries recorded the gospel in the language of the pygmies. Hundreds of records were made and played to this tribe. The response was extraordinary. These nomadic people heard the good news in their own language, the Holy Spirit worked, and they were wonderfully converted.

The degree of commitment and faith in this tribe

was so unusual that Gospel Recordings decided to do some research. What had brought about such a response? Certainly it wasn't just the recordings.

When they discovered how this sickly young girl had prayed in faith for so many years, they concluded this had to be the reason. Her prayers had advanced the gospel among these pygmies twenty years after her death. In God's time the answer had come down to earth. She had prayed from what was on God's heart, and He had brought it into being.[11]

When we pray, some answers come immediately. Others require waiting on our part, especially when we are praying for ourselves or the unreached peoples of the world. Changed lives require time — that is the way God works.

Jesus taught His disciples the importance of perseverance in Luke 18:1: "That they should always pray and not give up."

Adoniram Judson was a man who prayed and persevered and labored in Burma. He went to Burma in 1824 at twenty-four years of age. He prayed day after day for God to change the course of that nation. He vowed he would not leave until the cross was planted there forever.

He persisted in prayer. After seven years one man became a disciple. After ten years Judson was mistreated, tortured, and imprisoned. His wife and child died. After sixteen years he had baptized more than one hundred converts. His second wife died, more children died, he nearly died. He continued to give much time to prayer. After forty years he died in Burma. At his death there were 63 churches, 163 missionaries and workers, and more than 7,000 converts in Burma. Judson had planted the cross in Burma forever. He claimed God's promise.[12]

Do you have this promise of God? Yes, you assuredly have it. Whether you neglect it or not, it is yours. Every believer has this promise.

But that's not the question to ask. The more pertinent question is, "Does the promise have you?" When the promise possesses you, Christ possesses you, and you will go anywhere, you will do anything, you will sacrifice, you will endure suffering, you will even die if necessary to spread the blessing to the peoples of the earth — and you will persevere in prayer to that end.

The promise possessed Christ. It drove Him

to the cross. His last words before dying were "It is finished." He had fulfilled the promise. His last words on earth before He ascended were "But you will receive power when the Holy Spirit comes on you; and you will be my witnesses in Jerusalem, and in all Judea and Samaria, and to the ends of the earth" (Acts 1:8). The promise possessed Him, and by the power of the Holy Spirit it would possess the apostles and Christians following them until they witnessed to the salvation of Christ to all peoples — to the ends of the earth.

You can be part of that mighty succession and plant the cross forever among people — like Adoniram Judson or the young girl who prayed and prayed for the pygmies. She didn't go anywhere, but her prayers did, and for all eternity she can rejoice before God with the "little people" she prayed into His kingdom.

Through believing and persevering prayer you can have a significant part in multiplying the joint heirs with Christ among the peoples of the earth. That is the challenge of Christ's Great Commission. As someone has put it — "This is not the Great *Suggestion.*" It is the last and most demanding

33

mandate from our Savior King—that we go and make disciples among all peoples.

Whatever you decide to do with your life from here on, be sure it includes claiming the promise of God—which puts you into the world-blessing business. It is yours to experience personally and to use in extending God's kingdom globally. Those who are claimed by the promise claim the promise more effectively.

For Reflection and Action

You can start right now to claim God's promise in prayer!

1. a. With what one specific characteristic of Christ (His mercy, love, courage, etc.) would you like God to strengthen you?

   b. Ask God to strengthen you with this characteristic so that you can be a blessing to the people in your local world.

2. a. What blessing from the life of Christ is already a strength in your life?

   b. How could you apply this blessing to influence someone else this week? Talk with God about this.

3. a. Ask God which of the peoples of the world you could begin praying for this week. For whom would He like you to start claiming His promise?

   b. How can you start finding out about some nation in the world so that you can pray with wisdom?

4. Finally, ask the Lord to write His promise on your heart until it grips you.

If you are interested in a prayer ministry for the unreached peoples of Asia, please write to:

The Navigators
U.S.I.M.G.
P.O. Box 6000
Colorado Springs, CO 80934

Notes

1. John R. W. Stott, "The Living God Is a Missionary God," in *You Can Tell the World*, ed. James Berney (Downers Grove, IL: InterVarsity Press, 1979), 11.
2. Stott, 16.
3. Dr. Ralph Winter, letter to author, July 18, 1990.
4. R. A. Torrey, *How to Pray* (Old Tappan, NJ: Spire Books, Fleming H. Revell Co., 1970), 41.
5. According to the U.S. Bureau of Census, in 2007, 56.6 percent of the 6.6 billion people in

the world lived in Asia.

6. India is home to 1.1 billion people as of 2007.

7. "Mission Frontiers," *Bulletin of the U.S. Center for World Mission*, vol. 12, nos. 1 and 2 (Pasadena, CA: January–February 1990), 19.

8. As of 2007, conservative estimates indicate there are upward of 60 million Christians in China.

9. Ralph Winter and David A. Fraser, "World Mission Survey," in *Perspectives on the World Christian Movement* (Pasadena, CA: William Carey Library, Institute of International Studies, 1981), 344. In 2007, there were an estimated 380 million Christians in Africa.

10. S. D. Gordon, *What It Will Take to Change the World* (Grand Rapids, MI: Baker Book House, 1981), 112; and *Quiet Talks on Prayer* (Old Tappan, NJ: Fleming H. Revell Co., 1903), 15, 82.

11. Warren and Ruth Myers, *PRAY: How to Be Effective in Prayer* (Colorado Springs, CO: NavPress, 1983), 143.

12. Edward Judson, *The Life of Adoniram Judson* (New York: Randolph & Co., 1883).

Changing Your Thought Patterns

GEORGE SANCHEZ

NAVPRESS

Editor's Note: *George Sanchez originally gave this message, "Changing Your Thought Patterns," in 1977 as part of a series on interpersonal relationships. In reintroducing this booklet to a new generation, our intent is to preserve the original language of this classic message. The use of male pronouns reflects the original setting in which this booklet was written.*

౨౨౨౨౨

GEORGE SANCHEZ was on staff with The Navigators for four decades. Prior to that he served with radio station HCJB in Quito, Ecuador. Before retiring from The Navigators, he served as a counselor and teacher presenting seminars and conferences around the world. After moving to Albuquerque, New Mexico, George ministered to businessmen and couples seeking to reach the unchurched. He currently lives in a retirement facility, where he continues to seek the Lord.

"I wish I could stop being impatient with my children!"

"What can I do to keep from feeling guilty and depressed?"

"How can I have victory over my negative imagination?"

As I counsel with people, questions and statements like these are constantly mentioned. What they are asking basically is, "How can I change? How can I bring my thoughts under control and develop new attitudes?"

Change — Who Needs It?

Experiences we have had, including those in childhood, make impressions on us. These experiences cause us to respond in certain ways to situations we face later in life. This is a common pattern for all of us. One person never experienced an outward manifestation of affection from his father, and now he struggles with a deep need for that kind of expression. Another was made to feel he could never do anything properly, so today he battles with a sense of uncertainty and inferiority. Another was deeply hurt by someone to whom he reached out, and now he finds it difficult to trust anyone. But there are also the positive experiences. Many people experienced love, acceptance, support, and encouragement as children. They are able, as life develops, to relate more easily to people and circumstances.

Where the patterns are negative and destructive, the person needs change so he can find release and experience a new freedom—freedom that comes from knowing the truth and how to apply it. "Then you will know the truth, and the truth will set you free" (John 8:32). Where the patterns have been positive and affirming, they can be developed and reinforced by utilization and specific, planned action.

The important fact to recognize is that our thought patterns and habits *can be changed* constructively, and we can experience release from reactions and responses that continually defeat us.

Hope for Change

Let's look at a typical pattern of thinking. First, we recognize that there is a need to change an attitude, whatever that attitude may be. Maybe it's an attitude toward an individual or situation. In order to change his attitude, the Christian resorts to prayer. He hopes his attitude will change as a result.

We have been instructed that the way to change is through the means of prayer. After we pray, somehow something is supposed to happen and our attitudes change. We may not say it that way, but there is the implication that some mystical process takes place and attitudes change when a person reads the Bible or prays.

We recognize that there is a certain truth to that concept. The Bible says it, so we know that there has to be truth in it. "How can a young man keep his way pure? By living according to your word" (Psalm 119:9). <u>God is the only One who can bring about real change in our thought patterns.</u> We must always keep that in mind.

However, people repeatedly struggle in vain for results in this pattern — they pray and ask for help but nothing happens. No change of attitude takes place. They continue to struggle with the same basic conflicts. When this happens a pattern of defeat begins.

Of course, the enemy takes advantage at this point and begins accusing, "You see, there must be something else wrong or this attitude would change." So people look deeper, pray harder, spend longer periods of time with the Lord, and still many of these attitudes don't change. This is a real issue which we are going to encounter continually in our relationships with people.

Basis for Change

In considering this, we want to be very careful to avoid any idea of a so-called "do-it-yourself" Christianity. We do not make the changes in our lives. Only *God* has the power to make deep inner changes. We want to emphasize that so there is no misunderstanding.

On the basis of Proverbs 4:23, "Watch over your heart with all diligence, For from it flow the springs of life" (NASB), and other Scripture, we encourage people to saturate their hearts—their minds basically—with the Word of God. We believe that the more saturation takes place, the more people's conduct and way of thinking are going to be affected. Again, this is a true concept. But to experience change, we must put into practice the truths with which we are saturating our minds.

Renewing the Mind

To begin to understand how this applies to the concept of changing our thought patterns, let's examine one little phrase from Paul, "Be transformed by the *renewing of your mind*" (Romans 12:2, emphasis added). Every one of us must seek to answer the all-important and practical question, "How do I renew my mind?"

Let's use a hilltop as an illustration. When rain falls on a hill, the water drains off. How does it drain off? In rivulets. Initially, they are just small rivulets, but each time rain falls, the rivulets cut deeper and deeper. They can become deep chasms.

Now let's compare these rivulets with thought patterns in our minds. The longer we think along any given line, the stronger that thought pattern becomes. Every time we react in a certain way, we reinforce that thought pattern. This is how habits are formed.

If we want to get rid of rivulets on a hill, we could take a bulldozer and cover them up. We could also build a little dam where the rivulet begins so that the next time it rains the rivulets will change course. While we can't cover up our thoughts with a mental bulldozer, we can build a dam in our minds when certain thoughts begin. We can refuse to think them. We can say, "I will not allow myself to think that."

Redirecting Our Thoughts

Building a dam in the mind, however, is not enough. That is, saying "no" is not sufficient by itself. We also need to provide a new course for our thinking. We should not just suppress thoughts; we should redirect them. We should change negative thought patterns into positive thought patterns.

We find a good illustration of this in Paul's words: "He who has been stealing must steal no longer, but must work, doing something useful with his own hands, that he may have something to share with those in need" (Ephesians 4:28). How does a thief stop being a thief? Is it just by not stealing anymore? Not quite. Certainly that is part of it. That's saying "no" to a negative, destructive habit. It's building the "dam." But it's not enough. In order to change, the thief is told to get a job and earn money honestly. Then he is to give to others in need so that perhaps they won't be tempted to steal. *Now the process is complete.* The negative habit has been dealt with by an act of the will which chooses to stop it. But the will must also choose to replace that with the corresponding constructive action in order that the change in thought patterns may be complete.

And so it becomes clear that to change these thought patterns we must do two things. First, we must build the dam; that is, refuse to allow wrong thoughts. Second, we must redirect the flow and develop a new way of thinking. Eventually the old patterns will fade. They may never disappear, but they will fade and will become less and less influential in controlling our thinking.⌐

We need to realize that this takes place by an act of the will, not by wishful thinking and not solely by devotional meditation and prayer. Meditation and prayer are necessary, but we must move beyond that to an act of the will.

"Put Off" and "Put On"

Paul gives us some helpful thoughts on the subject: "Set your minds on things above" (Colossians 3:2). This is a declarative statement that involves an act of the will. You set your mind. He continues, "Put to death . . . whatever belongs to your earthly nature: sexual immorality, impurity, lust, evil desires" (verse 5), "You must rid yourselves" (verse 8), and "Put on" (verse 12, NASB). Changing thought patterns is not just "putting away" by building dams, but also "putting on" by building new patterns. It is not just suppressing, but redirecting our thoughts into healthy, positive ways of thinking.

What does "put to death" (verse 5) mean? The old thought patterns do not just die naturally. It would be great if they did, and we never again had this desire or that temptation. But because "the heart is more deceitful . . . and is desperately sick" (Jeremiah 17:9, NASB) and lusts against the Spirit, these battles go on continually. Therefore, the statement "put to death" requires a continual action. We must put old thought patterns to death every time they rear their heads. We cannot just put immorality to death and then no longer have immoral thoughts. They will continue to come up, and every time they do we have to stop them right at the headwaters with that dam. *Every time!* The more times we put those wrong thoughts to death and put on the new ones, the less our thoughts will tend to flow in the wrong direction.

Paul commands us to develop healthy, positive, spiritual ways of thinking (Colossians 3:12). We are to "put on" certain positive thought patterns as we "put off" the wrong ones. These two steps are essential if there is to be genuine change. We have looked at the illustrations of the changed thief (Ephesians 4:28). In the same passage Paul gives another helpful illustration of "putting off" and "putting on." He states that the liar is to stop (put off) lying but immediately reminds us that he must speak (put on) the truth (4:25). Not only does the liar stop lying, but he begins telling the truth. The two steps are clear — "put off" and "put on."

Crucified with Christ

Paul deals with this concept in his letter to the Romans (chapters 6–8). It helps to have some one-word titles for these passages. Romans 6 describes our *provision*. We have been delivered from the power of sin. "Our old self was crucified with him so that the body of sin might be done away with, that we should no longer be slaves to sin" (verse 6). "Because anyone who has died has been freed from sin" (verse 7). "Sin shall not be your master" (verse 14). "You have been set free from sin" (verse 18). *Provision* has been made so that we might overcome the power of sin.

Struggle is the key word in chapter 7. We struggle all the time. We struggle about how to get the provision of chapter 6 into our lives. The solution is the Lord Jesus Christ (verse 25). He is always the final answer. We all believe this. We preach sermons on it. We teach it. But too often we have not told people how to experience it in a practical way.

Chapter 8 gives us the *solution*. One phrase is repeated several times. Different versions state it in different ways, but the idea is the same. They all refer to "setting the mind." "Those who are according to the flesh *set their minds* on the things of the flesh, but those who are according to the Spirit, [*set their minds* on] the things of the Spirit. For the *mind set* on the flesh is death, but the *mind set* on the Spirit is life and peace, because the *mind set* on the flesh is hostile toward God" (verses 5-7, NASB, emphasis added).

Add to that these words of Paul, "Fix *your thoughts* on what is true and good and right. *Think about* things that are pure and lovely, and dwell on the fine, good things in others. *Think about* all you can praise God for and be glad about" (Philippians 4:8, TLB, emphasis added).

There, in essence, is the whole concept of what is commonly called the power of positive thinking: "Fix your thoughts." It is a statement of command which requires a response of the will—to fix our thoughts — to set our minds on these things.

The practical application of this concept is this: "Continue to work out your salvation with fear and trembling, for it is God who works in you to will and to act according to his good purpose" (Philippians 2:12-13). Note, it says "work out" not "work for" your salvation. We can compare this to a builder who has a set of plans that he must work out in order to do his job. In the same way we have been given "plans" regarding the Christian life that we are now responsible to "work out"; in other words, to put spiritual truth into action through obedience.

This verse presents the chronological process of the effective outworking of Romans 6–8. Another version states, "For God is the Energizer within you, so as to will and to work for His delight" (verse 12, MLB).

Our Responsibility

A light switch can be used to illustrate the Christian's responsibility in this process. As the light switch is moved, it turns the light on and off. That switch connects to a wire that goes through the house and out to a power line that eventually goes to a generating plant. Millions of volts of electricity are being produced there. The source of energy is enormous. The power comes through the lines to the wall switch. Whether the light is illuminated by the electrical energy depends on the position of the switch. The switch is a circuit breaker.

In the same way, what happens in the first part of Paul's statement determines whether the energy in the second part comes into our lives. Continually working out our salvation has to do with what we think—what we fix our thoughts on, what choices of will we make. In effect Paul says, "You do your part. You do what you know is right, then God will energize you to accomplish the right choice you make." This means we should renew our thoughts and not allow them to continue following negative patterns. Thus we are turning the "switch" on for God's energy to flow whenever we choose not to allow wrong thoughts to continue. This is difficult and requires personal discipline.

Ingrained Thought Patterns

Thought patterns are so ingrained that we don't recognize the stimulus that sets them off. And before we know it, one of our old thought patterns is off and running downhill. We respond to it as fast as a snap of the fingers. For example, when we hear the word "fireplace," we immediately see an image — good, bad, or indifferent. The words "ocean beach" immediately bring a specific picture to mind. These words are stimuli that induce an immediate thought pattern.

In the same way, there are many things that "trigger" or set off wrong thought patterns. We need to ask God to alert us through His Holy Spirit the minute these negative thought patterns begin.

That is all we can legitimately ask Him to do. When we ask God to change our thought patterns, we are asking Him to do something for which He has already said we are responsible.

Interpersonal Conflicts

Let's consider conflict in an interpersonal relationship as an illustration. One person says, "I have prayed for months, literally, for love for that person, but I just can't love him." However, when God says we are to do something, it is never a question of "can't" but "won't." God commands us to love others, whether or not they are our enemies, whether or not they have mistreated us. We are to love each other. No matter how we feel, God commands that we demonstrate the qualities of love (1 Corinthians 13:4-7) by an act of our will in obedience to that command. <u>As we act in obedience, our feelings will respond accordingly.</u> "A new commandment I give you: Love one another" (John 13:34). <u>The issue is not "can't" but "won't."</u>

There are many similar areas in which we often find ourselves asking God to change something when He has told us what to do. He tells us clearly that it us our responsibility to *fix our thoughts* and *"set our minds."* We have the right to ask God to alert us to the beginning of that negative thought pattern, but as soon as He alerts us, then the responsibility to take action is ours.

Example for Men

One of the areas that men have a great deal of difficulty with is their eyes—what they look at. We teach men that it is their responsibility to control their eyes. And while that emphasis may be proper, it presents a problem. The problem is that we are asking them to suppress a normal reaction. The Bible refers specifically to this. We are told in the words of the Lord Jesus that if a man looks on a woman to lust after her, he has committed adultery in his heart. Jesus didn't say it was wrong to look at a woman. He said it was wrong to look and lust. There is a difference.

Jesus never condemned seeing what normally crosses our line of sight, even when it's an attractive woman. Yet, we condemn it. We ask a man to act contrary to normal reaction, producing an immediate conflict. The moment a man looks at anything that might cause lust, he feels guilty. It is as though he shouldn't see or is supposed to wear blinders. It produces a tremendous amount of frustration.

What we should do is help men realize that looking at someone or something that is attractive is normal. However, how a man handles his subsequent thoughts is important. If he allows himself to dwell on lustful desires for that person or thing, according to Jesus, he is sinning. But I would emphasize that the same stimulus can be used to produce a positive response as well as a negative one.

Years ago when I began to realize this, I learned for the first time how to have real victory in this area of my own thought life. I remember how revealing and liberating it was. Whenever I would find myself looking at an attractive woman who could have generated wrong thoughts, I would admit them and control them by saying, "Thank You, Lord. Thank You that I am healthy, that I have normal responses, that I am made the way You intended me to be made, and thank You for a wonderful wife with whom I can enjoy what You have given me."

It only took a split second, but a dam was built and a new positive channel was constructed. It happened very quickly. By the grace of God, that has become a thought pattern now.

If I were a single man I would say the same thing, but the last phrase would read, "And thank You that in Your own time You will allow me the privilege of enjoying this part of my life, if that is Your plan for me." In either case, the principle is the same; that is, utilizing the same stimulus that could produce negative thoughts to produce positive responses instead by choosing that which I am going to allow my mind to think about.

I did not suppress those feelings. I did not say, "Come on, George, you are not supposed to think that way." That only reinforces the negative response I am trying to overcome. *Suppression reinforces negativism.* Sublimation or redirection reinforces a positive replacement of that negative thought. So, the same stimuli can produce positive results if we are alert to catch them the moment our thoughts begin a negative pattern. We do this by building a "dam" by saying no to the destructive thought and yes to a positive, constructive alternative.

Building the Dams

This is where Scripture comes in. Verses or concepts of Scripture can be used to build these dams which check our thinking. The next time that same thing stimulates our thinking we shouldn't say, "Don't think that way," but instead we should tell ourselves, "Don't think that way; *think this way.*" This redirects those thought patterns into positive directions. "Fix your thoughts on what is true and good and right" (Philippians 4:8, TLB).

If we do what God requests (Philippians 2:12),

then He promises to energize us (verse 13). We submit our wills to His. We decide by an act of the will not to continue in the old patterns but to let Him change us. He promises to do that. All we do is throw the switch by saying no to wrong thoughts and yes to the right ones. Then the energy from His enormous source of power flows through us and energizes us to do the very thing we want to do and that He wants us to do. Thus, it is not by our efforts that this is accomplished. *He produces the change, but we must make the choice.*

Dealing with Our Feelings

Let's look at another personal example. I found that in my relationship with my wife, Florine, I am not beyond feeling impatient. I never will be. As long as I am in this body and have the heart of flesh that I have, I am going to have these tendencies. But I find now that I am able to recognize these impatient feelings.

Speaking of feelings, I think it's important to understand a few things about them. It seems to me there is an emphasis that says, "Christians shouldn't have certain feelings." As a result, many sincere people find themselves struggling with guilt because they still have feelings they are told they shouldn't have. Feelings are normal to every human being. In themselves they are neither good nor bad. They simply are. We all experience them — anger, resentment, envy, jealousy, defensiveness, lust, and others. These are part of the temptations spoken of by Paul (1 Corinthians 10:13). The important thing is what we do with these feelings. A follower of Christ is not to be controlled by his feelings. This is what Proverbs 25:28 refers to as self-control.

Well then, how do we handle these feelings? This triad should help answer that:

1. *Our emotions respond.* As we've seen, we all have feelings that are set off by a variety of stimuli. It's important that we admit these feelings. It is destructive to try to deny or suppress them. But, as followers of Christ, we must not be controlled by these initial reactions.

2. *Our intellects (minds) evaluate.* We are responsible to "set our minds" and think through our emotional responses and their possible results. It is at this point that the Bible is so important. The more we know of what the Bible says, the more

24

truth we have by which to evaluate our reactions. This will also help us know what to do with the feelings we are experiencing.

3. *Our wills choose.* Having had the initial reaction and having evaluated, we now must choose our course of action. *Here is the crucial step!* Our evaluation may have told us that our feelings (reactions) are not biblical — they are neither constructive nor loving. In spite of this we may choose to act on the basis of feelings. This would be an immature response and behavior. It is also disobedience and sin (James 4:17). However, the mature choice, the one we have been discussing in order to change our thought patterns, is to heed the evaluation and act responsibly, even though our feelings might be otherwise.

One added word of caution. Sometimes after having submitted our will to God and disciplined ourselves to set our mind, we might become confused and fatigued when we don't experience the change we desire. In such cases, it is advisable to seek a mature, godly friend or biblical counselor to whom we can freely express our thoughts and feelings. There may be a need for other significant changes in our lifestyle, patterns of relationships, compulsive behavior or confusion in equating desires with needs. Talking and praying with such a person helps clarify issues and guides us in making wise choices and changes, both in lifestyle and thought patterns.

Now back to my feelings of impatience. When I recognize them, I admit them to God, myself, and Florine, so that she might understand and even give me added support. Then, by an act of my will, I determine, with God's help, to demonstrate patience because that is what love is. "Love is patient, love is kind" (1 Corinthians 13:4). I have found that as quickly as I do that, God energizes me to be patient! I have been surprised to see the distinct change that takes place from one brief moment to another. It is not because of my ability, but because I choose to submit my will to God's will. As a result, God energizes me.

Jesus Christ, Our Sufficient Rescuer

Paul is right when he refers to Christ as the One "who will rescue me from this" (Romans 7:24). The Lord Jesus Christ is the One. But first we must be willing to change our thought patterns — we must set our minds, fix our thoughts on what is true and good and right, and submit our wills to His. In other words, we must do our part. Then God can release the energy that He wants to give us to accomplish His purpose.

Many Aspire
Few Attain

WALTER A. HENRICHSEN

NAVPRESS

Editor's Note: Many Aspire, Few Attain *was originally published in 1975. In reintroducing this booklet to a new generation, our intent is to preserve the original language of this classic message. Scripture references in the King James Version, the use of male pronouns, and references to the Vietnam War reflect the original setting in which this booklet was written.*

ᘐᘐᘐᘐ

WALT HENRICHSEN served with The Navigators for many years and in 1977 left to begin working with business and professional men. He is married to Leette, and they have four children.

There's a war on today. We are no longer fighting in Vietnam, but we are engaged in a war that is far greater than that war—a war in which Vietnam was only a symptom. "We wrestle not against flesh and blood, but against principalities, against powers, against the rulers of the darkness of this world, against spiritual wickedness in high places" (Ephesians 6:12). This spiritual warfare is probably intensifying rather than receding.

When I was at Wycliffe Bible Translators' jungle camp in 1961 and 1962, we used to go on survival hikes. I loved camping out in the jungle. We would build a campfire and sleep around it in our lean-tos. We built a big fire because fire drove the wild animals deep into the jungle. But if you happened to wake up during the night as the campfire dwindled down, you would observe that the lower it got, the braver the animals became and the closer to the camp they crept. They formed a circle around the camp, and you could see those pairs of eyes looking at you from the forest. It was an incentive to throw a few more logs on, not so much because the night was cold as because you didn't know what was behind those eyes.

[In many respects, that's what is happening today in American evangelical Christianity. As the fires of evangelical Christianity grow dim, as biblical preaching diminishes across the nation, and as people give themselves more and more to sin, greed, the affluent life, permissiveness, and other selfish pursuits, the eyes of the evil one come closer and closer into the camp.]

Today, probably because we have abandoned the puritan ethic and have given ourselves over to the fruits of existentialism, we can see the forces of evil encroaching on our camp in a way we haven't seen in the past fifty years. The occult, witchcraft, Satan worship, and all these manifestations are very, very real. There *are* demons; there *are* demon-possessed people; there *is* sorcery. When you begin to play with astrology, Ouija boards, and similar things, you're giving expression to something which is not the figment of man's imagination, but that is warned against throughout the Bible. Because of this we live not only in perilous days but in days of unprecedented opportunity. The one glimmer of hope is that "where sin abounded, grace did much more abound" (Romans 5:20).

But the Devil is like a roaring lion, and his objective is to devour us. He is devouring through dope. He is devouring through loose living. He is devouring through people giving themselves to wrong goals and objectives.

Involvement in this spiritual warfare is a voluntary thing. It's our choice. In ancient Israel, before going to war, the officers said to the people, "What man is there that is fearful and fainthearted? let him go and return unto his house, lest his brethren's heart faint as well as his heart" (Deuteronomy 20:8). Involvement in spiritual warfare is voluntary as well.

The apostle Paul writes that a soldier must

7

endure suffering and hardship if he plans on getting into the battle (2 Timothy 2:3). The spiritual battle is a battle for keeps. Don't enter it unless you plan on winning. Don't enter it unless you plan on giving your life totally to it. Don't enter it unless you plan on suffering and enduring hardship because your adversary the Devil and his legions of demons play dirty. They fight rough. They give no quarter.

But Christ in you is greater than he that is in the world (1 John 4:4). And you are on the winning side. You can take refuge and consolation in that, but it is dirty, rough warfare — and the deeper you get into it, the meaner and nastier it gets. Men come and go, and the attrition rate in the Christian life is absolutely horrendous. In the final analysis, many aspire but few attain. Many begin well, but precious few end well.

You can climb on the shelf and render yourself ineffective for God in many ways. You can sign peace treaties with Satan and let him go his way while you go yours. Satan is willing to hold the ladder for any individual who wants to climb on the shelf for God. It is your choice.

It is relatively easy to recruit collegians because

they are at an idealistic age. They have a whole adventuresome life ahead of them. Everything looks like it's filled with opportunity. Collegians hate mediocrity. If there's one thing they want, it's idealism — idealism expressed in a better way of life.

That's why collegians rally around the banner that seeks to destroy the establishment. The establishment has compromised. The establishment has gotten fat with self-interest. The best thing to do from the idealist's point of view is to burn it down and start over. The average collegian is looking for a cause, for a flag to follow, for something to which he can give his life.

Recruiting the collegian to the spiritual battle is fairly easy. But it's a long uphill climb afterward. And the older a person gets, the more he feels like quitting. Victory is always in the future. It's not just around the corner.

Victory doesn't come by burning down a building. Victory doesn't come by having a law or two rescinded. Victory doesn't come when the university changes its ways. These are all symptoms.

The spiritual battle will take the rest of your life.

It will consume every ounce of your energy.

I talk to men in their thirties, forties, and fifties who were giving themselves to this cause when they were in their twenties. When they ask what I'm giving my life to and I respond it's the conquering of the world for Jesus Christ, their attitude toward me becomes very benevolent. A benign look comes across their faces and they pat me on the back and say, "Well, bless your heart, that's idealism for you." When you get that reaction, you've just met a person who has aspired but not attained. You have met a person who started well and ended poorly. You have met a man who began like you began and yet somewhere down the road has opted for mediocrity.

Most Christians do the same thing. The cares of the world, the deceitfulness of riches, and the lust of other things enter in, choking the Word. Their lives become unfruitful. They begin to give themselves to wall-to-wall carpeting, foam rubber, push buttons — to the acquisition of things. They begin to think in terms of retirement, pensions, the stock market, and wealth. They become encumbered with junk and are happily involved in it.

If you don't want to become a person who has aspired but not attained, you are going to have to make some resolutions in your own soul. You cannot give yourself or your enemy any quarter. Paul was concerned about his walk with God, "lest that by any means, when I have preached to others, I myself should be a castaway" (1 Corinthians 9:27).

As a Christian in the battle, like Paul, you're in the business of preaching to others. And like Paul, it is necessary to plan on not being a castaway. Let me suggest some ways you can avoid becoming one. This list is not exhaustive, and the items on it are not necessarily in the order of their importance.

1. Have a heart for God.

"One thing have I desired of the LORD, that will I seek after; that I may dwell in the house of the LORD all the days of my life, to behold the beauty of the LORD, and to enquire in his temple" (Psalm 27:4).

David writes, "One thing I . . . seek," not, "These forty things I dabble at." Moses said, "Thou shalt love the LORD thy God with all thine heart, and with all thy soul, and with all thy might" (Deuteronomy 6:5). With everything you've got. Now stop and evaluate. Do you have a real heart for God? Do you love Him with everything you have in you? Do you find that your life is consumed with the desire to follow Him? I'm not referring to emotionalism or sentimentality. I'm talking about a resolute spirit. Somewhere along the way have you said, "Oh, God, I will follow You with all of my heart and with all of my soul and with all of my mind"?

There are many Christians, but there are very few godly people. And there is a big difference between the two. Long before I was married I prayed, "Lord, if You ever want me to get married, I don't want a Christian girl. I want a godly woman. 'Favour is deceitful, and beauty is vain: but a woman that feareth the LORD, she shall be praised' (Proverbs 31:30). Lord, that's what I want. A woman who loves God."

The first thing you need to do to avoid becoming a castaway is to love God with everything you have.

2. Hate sin.

"Abhor that which is evil; cleave to that which is good" (Romans 12:9).

Close your eyes for a moment and think of something that really nauseates you. That feeling is the word Paul is using when he says "abhor." God wants you to view sin like you view the thing you're thinking about right now. That's what God wants your attitude to be. You can hardly contain yourself. You almost begin to gag you hate it so badly.

Do you have a hatred for sin? Do you find that you abhor that which is evil? Everyone is plagued with some sin, but some Christians don't hate evil. As a matter of fact, they have little pet sins they embrace. They play with them and pet them. No one else may even know about them except God.

Have you ever thought about what people will do in the presence of the living God that they would never do in front of other people? There are things that you'll do in God's presence that you won't do in front of anyone else. Isn't that true? You'll think thoughts and commit acts in the quietness and privacy of your own room or your own life that you'd never think of doing in front of another person.

God says, "I want you to hate sin. Abhor it." If there are sins you have embraced, if you have allowed them to rule in your life, if you play with them — if you have never dealt the victory blow to them even though the power has been given to you and all you have to do is appropriate it — there's no way you'll survive the battle. You don't want to give up the sin because you enjoy it. There's no way you're going to make it if you don't, though. You're going to be one of the casualties.

3. Hunger for the Word.

"As newborn babes, desire the sincere milk of the word, that ye may grow thereby" (1 Peter 2:2).

The third way that you can become a casualty in spiritual warfare is by not having a hunger for God's Word. Throughout the Bible the importance of hiding the Word of God in your life is emphasized. "Let the word of Christ dwell in you richly" (Colossians 3:16). "Thy words were found, and I did eat them" (Jeremiah 15:16). "Thy word have I hid in mine heart, that I might not sin against thee" (Psalm 119:11). "For the word of God is quick, and powerful, and sharper than any twoedged sword" (Hebrews 4:12). Your only chance of survival is to take the Word of God and to hide it in your life. The Word cleanses. The Scriptures give you the life and character of Jesus Christ. The Word of God gives you power. The Word gives you the ability to do the will of God.

How well are you hiding the Word of God in your life? Has the Word become perfunctory for you? Are you doing Bible study, or are you studying the Bible? There's a big difference between the two. Most people do Bible study. Are you really giving yourself to studying the Bible?

I can fill in Bible study blanks in about forty-five minutes, but it takes me between ten and fifteen hours to really study the chapter. I can show up with forty-five minutes preparation. I can have the blanks all filled in, I can participate, and I can make it look pretty good. I have done my Bible study, but I have not studied the Bible.

How do you evaluate yourself in terms of studying the Bible? Are you hiding the Word in your life? Do you find that you hunger for it? Do you find that you have a "sweet tooth" for the Word? Is it honey and milk to your lips? Do you find that you love to drink deep at its well? If not, then there is no way you're going to make it. You're going to be one of those who begin well and end poorly. There's no way you can survive.

I run across people again and again in the Christian community who say, "Well, you know, Henrichsen, you can't be legalistic in these things." And that's right. Or, "You know I find that when I am around Navigators, they kind of squeeze me into their mold." I know exactly what they are talking about. "There hath no temptation taken you but such as is common to man" (1 Corinthians 10:13). But, if you have that attitude, remember it's not your Bible study leader's problem, it's not your Navigator representative's fault. It's your fault. It's because of the coldness of your heart. It's because you have no hunger for the Word of God. Yours is not really a legalistic problem; it is a spiritual problem.

You can solve the problem of allowing yourself to be trapped in the web of method rather than using method as a key to unlock treasures. First, spend a lot of time in the Word. Second, meditate and think on the Word of God instead of doing the perfunctory ritual of the form. You can really make it live. Third, apply it to your life. After all, the Word of God was given primarily to change your life, not to increase your knowledge.

Make sure you are applying the Word of God.

4. Trust God.

"Trust in the LORD with all thine heart; and lean not unto thine own understanding" (Proverbs 3:5).

There are going to be times in your life when the living God, to use a gambler's term, is going to take all of the blue chips, push them right in the middle of the table, and say, "Friend, we're going for broke on this one. Let's see how you're doing in your Christian life." More often than not, people push all kinds of panic buttons on the console and punch out.

If you really want to walk with God, then you have to learn to trust Him. And if you want to learn to trust Him, you've got to learn to trust Him in the little things so that when the big things come along, you have established a habit of it. Your faith will be tested. You are no greater than your forefathers. The day is going to come when the bottom is going to drop out, the roof is going to cave in, and somebody's going to say, "Cheer up, it's going to get worse." And sure enough, you'll cheer up and it will get worse.

Are you trusting God in the little things? How about your finances? It's tough to really trust God in this area, to give when you can't afford it. There's no faith involved in giving when you can afford it. Faith comes when you give what you cannot afford.

There are many things you can do in your life without faith. Without faith you can get married. Without faith you can have a home. Without faith you can become a millionaire. Without faith you can live a normal, relatively happy life. But there's one thing you cannot do without faith. "Without faith it is impossible to please him" (Hebrews 11:6). If you're planning on pleasing God, you've got to walk by faith.

God is in control of this world. And all He wants from you is intelligent cooperation. Boiled down to one word, that simply means *trust*. Many will never make it simply because they cannot muster up enough courage and faith in their souls to really trust Him when the going gets rough.

5. Burn bridges and ships.

"No man, having put his hand to the plough, and looking back, is fit for the kingdom of God" (Luke 9:62).

You'll never attain if you refuse to burn your boats. When Spanish conquistador Hernando Cortez took his men to Mexico, his objective was to march on Mexico City and conquer Montezuma. When he landed at Vera Cruz, he put all his men on the beach and sent demolition teams out to destroy their ships. As the men stood on the shore watching the ships burn and sink, they realized that there was no turning back. They were in Mexico for life.

Have you burned your ships? Have you taken whatever avenues of retreat you have — I'm talking about mental things — and burned them? If you are a college student, how about your education? You began in college or the university with a goal. You wanted to get a degree to do something. There's nothing wrong with education. There's nothing wrong with getting your degree, but there is something wrong if that becomes an end in and of itself. Have you given your degree, your vocational goals, and the direction of your life back to God? If your university is a mission field for you to accomplish the will of God, good. If the university is a means for you to accomplish your own selfish ends, you are living in sin, and God wants you to burn that boat.

Perhaps you have a boyfriend or a girlfriend. Have you given him or her back to God? Many people have bitten the dust on this one. They've never made it simply because they were unwilling to commit this area of their lives to God.

Some time ago some parents asked me to talk to their eighteen-year-old daughter. I'll call her Sharon. She was a beautiful young girl — sweet and attractive. Sharon was in love with a fellow. She wanted to marry him. I asked her if it was the will of God. She said, "No." I asked her if she was willing to give him back to God. She said, "No." We talked about it until two or three in the morning. But Sharon had made up her mind that she was going to marry his man, and she did.

About a year and half later I was talking to her folks, and I asked how Sharon was. They kind of dropped their heads and said, "Oh, fine." I asked what she was doing. "Well, she's got a baby girl. She's living in an apartment by herself. Her husband left her. She's divorced and she doesn't know what to do."

"Be not deceived; God is not mocked: for whatsoever a man soweth, that shall he also reap" (Galatians 6:7). The only way you can avoid that terrible, terrible plight is to burn your ships and to let God make those decisions.

6. Beware the road of no return.

"But the LORD was wroth with me for your sakes, and would not hear me: and the LORD said unto me, Let it suffice thee; speak no more unto me of this matter" (Deuteronomy 3:26).

In this passage Moses is making his closing remarks and reviewing his life with the children of Israel. Remember, he spent the first forty years in the palace, the second forty years squeezing sand between his toes, and the third forty years wandering around the wilderness with a rebellious people, burying his own generation. Can you imagine the number of funerals Moses had to attend? Forty years of burying his own generation, and there were a slug of them. Now he's reviewing his life and he says, "But the LORD was wroth with me for your sakes, and would not hear me."

Why was God angry? In the wilderness the children of Israel complained about water. God told Moses to strike the rock and water would come out. Moses struck the rock and sure enough, the water came out. The second time that the same incident occurred, God said to speak to the rock. But Moses was angry because of the rebelliousness of the people, and he struck the rock. The water came out, but God said, "Moses, you are through. You will not go into the promised land." Moses had lived over one hundred years of his life with one thing on his mind—getting into that promised land. Over one hundred years! And now he couldn't go in because of one dumb mistake. Just one, not two or three, not five—one! Paul tells us that the rock was Jesus Christ, and He should be smitten only once (1 Corinthians 10:4). Because of that, God said, "You will not go into the promised land."

Now Moses pled with God, "Lord, change Your mind. Lord, please give me another chance." But, "The LORD was wroth with me for your sakes, and would not hear me: and the LORD said unto me, Let it suffice thee; speak no more unto me of this matter."

In other words, "Moses, don't bring the matter up again." And when God says, "Don't bring up the matter again," it is best not to bring up the matter again.

The sixth reason why people don't make it is that they enter the road of no return. "If we confess our sins, he is faithful and just to forgive us our sins, and to cleanse us from all unrighteousness" (1 John 1:9) is not the answer to some wrong decisions.

If you don't make certain decisions in the center of God's will, you will automatically become disqualified from the race.

7. Avoid an independent spirit.

The seventh reason why people will never make it is because they have an independent spirit. They are mavericks, loners. They want to serve God, but in their way. Perhaps you are like the fellow I asked about the episcopal form of government. He answered, "Well, I'm against bishops unless I can be one."

A lot of Christians have that attitude. They are against spiritual authority and leadership unless they *are* the authority and the leader. But God says He will not give you that which is your own until you have been part of that which is another man's (Luke 16:12).

The prophet Elijah, as he was about to be taken out of this world, said to his follower Elisha, "Tarry here" (2 Kings 2:2). Elisha answered, "No way, friend. Where you go, I go. There's no way you can get rid of me." Where is the guy or gal you have committed yourself to in an Elijah/Elisha relationship? Where is your Elijah? Where's the person who you are going to lock into by the will of God and go for broke with? You might say, "Well, God is my teacher. He can speak to me as easily as He can speak through someone else. After all, doesn't the Bible say that you shouldn't be lord over the flock and you shouldn't be like little tin gods?"

That's true. Nobody is your lord except Jesus. But I'm not referring to lordship. I'm talking about an independent spirit.

Do you remember the argument that Dathan, Korah, and Abiram gave Moses (Numbers 16)?

"You take too much upon yourself, Moses. God can speak to us just as easily as He can speak to you. We don't need to follow you. Man alive! Don't we believe in the priesthood of believers? Don't our prayers get through to God? Can't God speak to us? After all, why should we follow your leadership?"

And Moses said, "Well, let's talk this over with God and see what He says."

"Okay, let's do it."

So they went to God and He said, "Moses, step aside and let Me show you what I think of that idea." So Moses stepped aside and God opened up the earth and Dathan, Korah, Abiram, and all that belonged to them fell in. God closed the earth back up and then sent fire that consumed the 250 men who were with them in rebellion.

Then God asked the children of Israel, "Any other questions?"

But Israel got mad at Moses and said, "Moses, you dirty rat, you sicced God on us!" Thousands more died of the plague that day because of their attitude.

God asked again, "Any more questions?" And the children of Israel said, "No. We got the point."

God does not hanker to an independent spirit. You can be a maverick, you can be a loner, and you can go your own way. It's up to you. But that is an awfully quick way to climb on the shelf.

8. Be wholehearted.

"And he did that which was right" (2 Kings 14:3). This passage refers to King Amaziah. But because one thing was lacking—his heart wasn't right—God couldn't use him. Within a short time Amaziah was dead.

Some Christians create the impression that they are doing God and their Christian organization a favor by being around—that God Almighty is about the luckiest of the lucky to have them on His team. Nothing could be further from the truth. Perhaps you have this attitude. Now God is delighted beyond words over the fact that you are His. He loves you with an everlasting love. But never deceive yourself into believing that you are doing either God or man a favor by being faithful.

It is easy to be wholehearted in the things you like doing, but it's hard to be wholehearted in the things you don't like doing. When I moved into a

Navigator home, one of my responsibilities every Saturday morning was to clean the bathroom in the master bedroom. I can remember being on my hands and knees over the toilet bowl with the cleanser and wondering to myself, *"Henrichsen, what in the world are you doing here? There are millions of places you could be rather than sitting here looking down inside a toilet."* It's hard enough to clean your own dirt, but it is even harder to clean other people's dirt.

How do you rate yourself in terms of your wholeheartedness in being a servant of God?

I don't mind being a servant of Jesus Christ. I revel in it. I don't mind you calling me a servant. But you know what I do mind? You treating me like a servant.

Can you be wholehearted when people treat you like a servant of the most high God and a servant of your fellow man?

9. Be faithful in the little things.

"He that is faithful in that which is least is faithful also in much: and he that is unjust in the least is unjust also in much" (Luke 16:10).

Many aspire but few attain because they are unfaithful in the little things. Lorne Sanny, president of The Navigators, has said that Charlie Riggs was one of the few men he ever worked with who could be counted on to carry through on a request. Lorne could check it off as being accomplished and never had to go back and see if it had been done. That challenges me tremendously.

Can people say that about you? When you are given an assignment, when somebody's asked you to do something, can they mark it off as being completed? No matter how small it is — whether it's picking up a couple of postage stamps or mailing a letter — when you have been asked to do something, can you be counted on to do it? Are you faithful in that which is least? Jesus said there is no way He is going to give you greater responsibilities till you've proven yourself faithful in the little things.

And when promotion does come, it doesn't come from men, it comes from God. "For promotion cometh neither from the east, nor from the west, nor from the south. But God is the judge: he putteth down one, and setteth up another" (Psalm 75:6-7).

10. Avoid the root of bitterness.

"Looking diligently lest any man fail of the grace of God; lest any root of bitterness springing up trouble you, and thereby many be defiled" (Hebrews 12:15).

The tenth reason many will never make it is because of envy, jealousy, and bitterness — a competitive spirit. A bitter spirit, a spirit of resentment, poisons not only you but others.

A root of bitterness is the result of real or supposed ill treatment. It does not make any difference. You can get just as bitter thinking people treated you badly as when they actually do treat you badly. Feeling hurt and sorry for yourself are bedfellows of bitterness. Self-pity is the other side of the coin of the root of bitterness. Have you ever felt sorry for yourself? Have you ever felt hurt over the way people have treated you? Then you are bordering on bitterness.

George Washington Carver once said, "I will never let another man ruin my life by making me hate him." Those are profound words. Because you see, when you hate, you destroy yourself.

[If God is God — and He is — then nobody can hurt you. Nobody. That simply means that any time you are angry with another person, it's not really the other person who you are angry with — it's God. God is the One who allowed that to happen in your life. Whenever circumstances go amiss and things don't go your way, when you get angry and become resentful and bitterness begins to creep into your heart, remember your complaint is *always* with God. Never with anyone else. There is no such thing as having a problem with another person. It doesn't exist. And bitterness will destroy you if you let it.]

11. Accept rebuke.

"For whom the Lord loveth he chasteneth, and scourgeth every son whom he receiveth" (Hebrews 12:6).

Some people never make it because they can't take rebuke. I don't mind God rebuking me. But the fact of the matter is that God uses other people. Solomon says, "He that refuseth instruction despiseth his own soul" (Proverbs 15:32). If you refuse to take instruction, you are despising your own soul.

Why? Because the rebuke that comes into your life is for your own good.

"Reprove not a scorner, lest he hate thee: rebuke a wise man, and he will love thee" (Proverbs 9:8). Don't reprove a scorner because he turns around and hates you. Reprove wise men because they will love you for it.

When was the last time someone rebuked you—the last time someone sat down and instructed you more perfectly in the way? If it has not been recently, it is because people don't consider you to be wise. They think you are a scorner. They are afraid if they rebuke you, you won't take it. Don't deceive yourself into believing that you haven't been rebuked lately because you haven't needed it. You need it. The question is, are you getting it? You can tell whether or not people think you are wise by how often they rebuke you.

Once when Warren Myers and I were doing Bible study together his application was to pray that God would send somebody into his life to rebuke him at least once a week. What a challenge! Want to pray that one?

12. Stay constant.

"Thus saith the LORD, Stand ye in the ways, and see, and ask for the old paths, where is the good way, and walk therein, and ye shall find rest for your souls. But they said, We will not walk therein. Also I set watchmen over you, saying, Hearken to the sound of the trumpet. But they said, We will not hearken. Therefore hear, ye nations, and know, O congregation, what is among them. Hear, O earth: behold, I will bring evil upon this people, even the fruit of their thoughts, because they have not hearkened unto my words, nor to my law, but rejected it" (Jeremiah 6:16-19).

Some people just want to be different — they don't want to be pushed into any particular mold. So they vacillate from one place to the next. For example, many people are excited about The Navigators when they first become involved. It's new, it's exciting, it's fresh. But then they become critical of the clichés and the traditions of the group. God's Word, on the other hand, is applicable for all time because it is timeless.

And what happens when a person wants change

for the sake of change is that he exchanges one mold for another. The beatniks of the fifties and the hippies of the sixties are examples of this. Desiring to be nonconformists, they created a new kind of conformity. And while God has created everyone individually and uniquely, He has also set standards and given the Christian instructions on how to be the kind of person who will survive the battle and be able to move forward for Christ.

13. Walk by faith.

In the beginning, living by faith has an excitement which is unlike anything else. But after a while, the novelty of it begins to wear off, and it begins to seem more desirable to have some security — to be able to count on something rather than trusting God all the time.

And then slowly things begin to become more important. What you have, rather than what God can provide, becomes your security. This can go to the extreme. For example, one woman did not like to have people in her home because they messed it up. If your home or any of your possessions become more important than people, then you are already out of the battle. God is interested in people. And when your security is in Him, what happens to things is not as important. If your rugs, sofa, and cut-glass bowls are more important than people, you will never qualify for the battle.

14. Keep up the heart for the battle.

"I beseech you therefore, brethren, by the mercies of God, that ye present your bodies a living sacrifice, holy, acceptable unto God, which is your reasonable service" (Romans 12:1).

If you get used to seeing God do miracles, you can cease to be thrilled and thankful. Things can become old hat.

You remember the story of the hare and the tortoise. The hare started out great, but he was sidetracked along the way because it was so easy — there was no question about succeeding. No big deal. The tortoise, on the other hand, just kept plugging along, recognizing that in order to win the race, he needed to put all his efforts into it. And he won. He kept his eye on the objective and did not allow himself to be distracted.

Like the race between the tortoise and the hare,

the battle which Christians face today needs to be won. It is for keeps. And also like the race between the tortoise and the hare, there are many potential distractions along the way. Have no doubt that Satan will try everything he can to take your eye off the objective and to disqualify you from the battle.

The fourteen suggestions listed here are ways Christians can avoid being taken out of the battle. Too often Satan is successful, and the Christian becomes a casualty. Thus, while many begin well, few end well.

While many aspire, few attain.

May you be one of those who attains.

More NavClassics from NavPress!

Born to Reproduce
Dawson Trotman
ISBN 978-1-60006-398-5 (5 pack)
ISBN 978-1-60006-407-4 (25 pack)

Changing Your Thought Patterns
George Sanchez
ISBN 978-1-60006-400-5 (5 pack)
ISBN 978-1-60006-410-4 (25 pack)

Claiming the Promise
Doug Sparks
ISBN 978-1-60006-401-2 (5 pack)
ISBN 978-1-60006-409-8 (25 pack)

How to Spend a Day in Prayer
Lorne C. Sanny
ISBN 978-1-60006-402-9 (5 pack)
ISBN 978-1-60006-411-1 (25 pack)

Many Aspire, Few Attain
Walter A. Henrichsen
ISBN 978-1-60006-403-6 (5 pack)
ISBN 978-1-60006-412-8 (25 pack)

Marks of a Disciple
Lorne C. Sanny
ISBN 978-1-60006-399-2 (5 pack)
ISBN 978-1-60006-408-1 (25 pack)

The Need of the Hour
Dawson Trotman
ISBN 978-1-60006-404-3 (5 pack)
ISBN 978-1-60006-413-5 (25 pack)

To order your pack of five or twenty-five, call NavPress at
1-800-366-7788, or log on to www.navpress.com.